"Edward O'Malley makes a valuable contribution to the on-going study of American generations and the cycles of history."
- Neil Howe, co-author of national bestseller *The Fourth Turning and Generations.*

American Renewal

D0863344

American Renewal

*A New Season of Optimism,
Cooperation and Community*

Edward O'Malley

Celtic Free Press
Seaside

American Renewal
A New Season of Optimism, Cooperation and Community

Celtic Free Press
1336 Luxton St.
Seaside, CA 93955

Library of Congress Cataloging-in-Publication Data is available

Paperback ISBN: 978-1-62747-280-7
Ebook ISBN: 978-1-62747-290-6

Printed in the United States of America

"The greatness in America lies not in being more enlightened than any other nation, but rather in her ability to repair her faults."

Alexis de Tocqueville, Democracy in America, 1835

This book is dedicated to my mother, Jean Byrnes O'Malley, who always encouraged me to follow my dreams and approached every day with gratitude, a positive attitude and boundless love and devotion for her children.

Contents

Preface

    I was inspired to write this book by my wife, Timi, during a vacation to Hawaii in 2017. I have been studying history, foreign affairs and social change all of my life and more extensively since 1997 when I first read *The Fourth Turning* by William Strauss and Neil Howe. Their book identifies a distinct, four-period cycle of social change in America that occurs over about eighty years and includes Crisis, High, Awakening, and Unraveling periods. Strauss & Howe trace the occurrence of this four-period cycle in great detail over five centuries of Anglo-American history in *The Fourth Turning*. They term the change to a new period in the cycle as a "turning," akin to what Pete Seeger described in his song *Turn, Turn, Turn*. At each turning there is a visible and abrupt shift in the mood of the country, usually marked by a significant event on a single day. I have been discussing this topic with people ever since 1997, so it was time to capture my thoughts in this book.

    They laid out a coherent rationale for an upcoming Crisis period in America that would immediately change the mood and direction of the country. That crisis soon occurred on September 11, 2001. I was further motivated to write this book after reading Bruce Springsteen's well-written autobiography *Born to Run* (named after his first hit album released in 1975*)*, which traces his career and the themes of his music along the same time periods of social change in America that Strauss and Howe described. The parallels were fascinating.

    Back in 1997, America was deeply embroiled in an intense "Unraveling" period, as Strauss and Howe called it. The country had seen a steady erosion in family life, trust in government, and social order since an "Awakening" period began in 1963. I grew up during the Awakening period, so events during that time made a strong impression on me. The start of the Unraveling period was marked with the election of an ebullient President Reagan in 1980, after his "Let's Make America Great Again" campaign. The country soon slipped into a deep recession following several years of high inflation.

While campaigning for re-election in 1984, Reagan had mistakenly interpreted the title of Bruce Springsteen's new album, *Born in the USA,* as validation for his new campaign theme of "Morning in America." What Reagan didn't realize was that *Born in the USA* was an unvarnished look at how middle-class Americans were suffering from the social and economic change of the past twenty years. It was more like "fall in America," and winter was coming. In his book, Springsteen relates his experience of growing up and coming-of-age in those years, while writing his poignant songs that captured those challenges, and working tirelessly on his own dream of achieving success.

> *Bruce Springsteen expressed how jobs had vanished from America and would not return, leaving towns impoverished in his 1984 song My Hometown.*

In the years between 1997 and 2001, I had seen examples of the shifts predicted by Strauss & Howe that would occur as we entered the crisis period. They postulated that the gap between gender roles narrowed during an Awakening period and widened during a Crisis period. That prediction came to mind as I read a *Wall Street Journal* article on February 14, 2000 titled "Why Boys and Girls Get Different Toys," explaining that the "gender neutral" marketing strategy was out. Kid marketers would now pitch single–sex products for each gender. For Millennials and Gen X, this may have seemed only natural, but they had not grown up when companies like Toys "R" Us and Mattel had been using a gender-neutral marketing approach since the 60's, coincident with the Awakening period and the women's movement push for equality. The article clearly indicated that the nearly forty-year trend was reversing.

Of much greater concern to me was the nature and implications of the Crisis period that they predicted was coming soon. They offered a range of plausible major events that might signal the end of the Unraveling period and usher in the start of a new Crisis period: a fiscal crisis, a major terrorist attack, total government shutdown, virus epidemic, or foreign-policy crisis. As a Baby Boomer, I grew up in a safe distance from America's previous Crisis period, but I was an avid reader of U.S. and world history. Although the stock-market crash on Black Tuesday in 1929 signaled the start of The Great Depression and the actual beginning of that crisis period, the single event that sticks in people's minds even more was the Japanese surprise attack on Pearl Harbor in 1941.

As I walked down the main street of Monterey in May, 2001 I stopped abruptly when I saw the old-style marquee of the Golden State Theater announcing the premier of the movie *Pearl Harbor,* starring Ben Affleck. I felt that the premier of this particular film was a vivid foreshadowing of the start of the new crisis period. The relevance of that film is even more significant to me as I began to write this book in May, 2017 on the north shore of Oahu near where the Japanese planes swarmed below the radar through the Wahiawa valley over the pineapple and sugarcane fields, enroute to their unsuspecting targets at Wheeler Air Field and then Pearl Harbor. I deeply believed that the start of a new crisis period was imminent.

Just four months later, the United States would begin the first Crisis period since the sixteen years between

1929 and 1945, which bracketed the Great Depression and World War II. Everyone remembers where they were on the morning of September 11, 2001 when four planes were hijacked by radical Islamists and deliberately flown into both towers of the World Trade Center, the Pentagon and a verdant field in southwestern Pennsylvania. On that day, the mood and lives of all Americans were instantly changed.

The social, political and economic problems that we had faced over the 40 years since President Kennedy was assassinated suddenly seemed irrelevant as the towers imploded on themselves and on the many souls within them. Families were devastated as fathers, mothers, sisters, brothers, sons, and daughters perished at the hands of a foreign enemy. This new crisis would call for Americans to work together to overcome a common problem, or in this case, a common enemy. Bumper stickers and window placards with "United We Stand" appeared everywhere. It was time to set aside differences and work together. And for a while, we did.

Since 9/11, we have witnessed the moods and attitudes of the country shift with each new crisis that emerged. We looked to heroes at home and abroad to reassure ourselves that we would be all right. Heroes are a crucial part of the social ethos during a crisis, both in real life and in popular culture such as films. Now, nearly sixteen years later, the U.S. will soon close the chapter on the worst Crisis period in nearly eighty years and lay the foundation for a new "High" period. This new High period will call on Gen X and Gen Y (Millennials) to lead the country in a more cooperative spirit towards an American renewal. Gen Z will serve as the dutiful executors of that strategy. A Crisis period begins and ends with a definitive and climactic event that will usher in the new High period. I believe that concluding event will be the Presidential election on November 3, 2020.

The purpose of this book is to explain Strauss and Howe's theory of generational cycles and the four periods that comprise it; Crisis, High, Awakening, and Unraveling. We will also examine the key events and social change that occurred in America during each of these periods since 1945. It is also to describe the unique generation that comes of age during a new turning and the persona or archetype that they embody. Finally, it is also to consider what that new High period may look like and the new generation that will help shape it. This new period will be an American Renewal, a period of greater optimism, cooperation, and community.

Introduction

This story is about much more than just the current crisis period. This is a journey through the experiences of four generations of Americans across a cycle of history that began in 1945 and will end around 2020, when the cycle will begin again. It is about the four distinct periods that make up that cycle – Crisis, High, Awakening, and Unraveling. It is to call out the unique, new generation that "comes of age" during these periods and how they shape the periods themselves.

Each of us is a member of a distinct generation, born during a specific era and shaped by the childhood events of that period. But the period in which we "come of age" is the one that defines us as a generation. The G.I. Generation is best known for first coming of age during the Great Depression and then later going off to fight in WWII. Baby Boomers are best known for the Awakening period from 1963 to 1980 and the social change they shaped during that time. I vividly remember sitting in my third-grade classroom on Friday, November 22, 1963, when the televisions in our classroom, normally used for French classes taught by our principal, were tuned in to one of the major networks who announced that President Kennedy had been shot. Our northern suburb of Chicago had many Irish and Italian Catholics who voted enthusiastically for Kennedy. Everyone was stunned. Teachers and children sobbed. Later, while in college in the late '70s, I felt the social ennui as the Awakening period was losing momentum and the mood discernably shifted when Ronald Reagan was elected President in 1980.

A generation is said to "come of age" sometime between the age of 18 and 21. We typically mark these "coming of age" milestones with high-school graduation

ceremonies and entering college for many. Table #1 below
identifies the six most recent generations in America and
their birth years, which span from 16 to 20 years. The birth
years for each generation in this book coincide with the
year of the major events that mark the start and the end
of each period. Individuals near the cusps of these dates
may likely self-identify as belonging to one generation or
another. Other authors and publications may show different
birth years for each generation. The social period (turning)
in which they came of age along with the years that that
period covered is also shown.

Figure I-1.

America's Generations	Generation's Birth Years	Generation's "Coming of Age"	Periods Years
G.I. (Greatest Gen)	1908 - 1924	Crisis	1929 - 1945
Silent Generation	1925 - 1944	High	1945 - 1963
Baby Boomers	1945 - 1963	Awakening	1963 - 1980
Gen X	1964 - 1980	Unraveling	1980 - 2001
Gen Y - Millennials	1981 - 2001	Crisis	2001 ~ 2020
Gen Z	2002 ~ 2020	High	2020 ~ 2038

It is important to note the size of each generation to
understand the impact that each has on society and culture
as a whole. As the overall population of the U.S. continues
to increase, each generation has grown larger than the
prior one, even as fertility birth rates have declined. The
population grew from 180 million in 1960 to over 280
million in 2000. So while the size of the Baby Boomer
generation was large at the time, Millennials will far eclipse
them in size. Gen Z is still being born as of 2018, but
should eventually match or exceed the Millennials in size at
the current pace of births, depending on the exact number
of years that Gen Z will span.

Figure I-2.

Generation	Year		Births	# of Years	Avg/Year
Baby Boomers	1945	1963	56,416	18	3,134
Gen X	1964	1980	58,932	16	3,683
Millennials	1981	2001	81,911	20	4,096
Gen Z*	2002	2020	57,121	13	4,394

*U.S. Census Data   *Gen Z through 2015 only*

One of the main themes we will explore is public trust in government and how this ebbs and flows with each period and each generation's coming-of-age. Public trust in government to do the "right thing almost always or most of the time" is currently near historic lows, according to the Pew Research Center, which has been tracking this indicator since 1958. John Gardner describes in his book *Self-Renewal* that "a society decays when its institutions and individuals lose their vitality."[1] He echoes de Tocqueville as well as the theme of cycles when he adds that "just as beliefs and values are susceptible to decay, so are they capable of regeneration."[2] Trust levels were 75-80% from 1958 until 1963, during the last High period. Trust began to fall after then in the wake of the Vietnam War, Watergate, and the social upheaval during the Awakening period. Trust finally hit a low point in 1980 but received a slight and temporary boost in the '80s during the Reagan administration, before dropping again during the first Bush administration. Trust soared to nearly 60% during the late '90s when the economy was booming, the Soviet Union had collapsed and thee was an absence of any major military conflicts. A national sense of unity after 9/11 helped send trust ratings higher, but quickly soured and plunged to 20% as the war in Iraq deteriorated amid realization of its false premise, the Great Recession roared through American homes, Hurricane Katrina slammed into New Orleans, and polarization plagued our government and media.

Figure I-3. Trust in Government

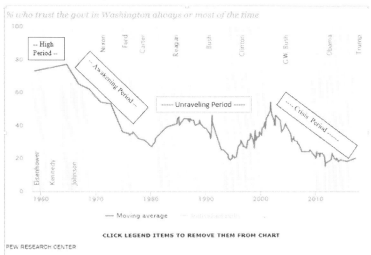

% who trust the govt in Washington always or most of the time

PEW RESEARCH CENTER

CLICK LEGEND ITEMS TO REMOVE THEM FROM CHART

Introduction to Cycles

But we have experienced these periods before. As Mark Twain is said to have quipped, "History doesn't repeat itself, but it does rhyme." Such does the period in a new cycle follow the rhythm of the same period in a previous cycle, but it is not a replica. The generation is new and reflects the modernity of its time, but echoes the persona of the generation from its same place in the previous cycle. Hence the persona of the millennial generation is being shaped by the current crisis period, similar to how the G.I. Generation's was shaped during the last crisis.

Pete Seeger expressed how cycles, expressed as seasons, were present in every part of life and repeated with time in his iconic 1959 song Turn, Turn, Turn.

These words first appeared in the Bible, Ecclesiastes 3:1-8, before American folk singer Pete Seeger used them in the anti-war song he wrote in the late 1950s. Having been blacklisted as a former member of the American Communist Party, Seeger wanted to write a song that would be difficult for people to ascribe to Communist ideology, while still voicing his dissent on social and political issues. The Bible seemed like a safe place to find one. *Turn, Turn, Turn* would become one of the classic "anthem" songs of the Baby Boomer generation after the Byrds performed it and it rose to the top of the Billboard charts in December, 1965. The lyrics poignantly capture the theme of this book, that social change is driven by the values and persona of each new generation, who bring a distinct "season" to the country -- and those four seasons repeat in a new cycle.

Cycles are part of our natural human existence. Just as the sun rises and falls each day, the seasons alternate from spring to summer to fall to winter, and back to spring again. Each spring may be quite different from those of previous years, but it bears essential similarities to all other springs. The cycles of social change that Strauss and Howe identified also follow the same pattern as our seasons and share their characteristics: High (spring), Awakening (summer), Unraveling (fall), and Crisis (winter).

Outside of nature, writers and historians have ascribed cycles to business (Keynes), politics (Schlesinger), foreign policy (Klingberg), and even Generations (Strauss & Howe). As Schlesinger pointed out in *The Cycles of American History* (1986), "The roots of cycles lie deep in the natural life of humanity, just as in organic nature."[3] He goes on to add that pure cycles are continuous and have an "internal" explanation. Thus, they are self-generating. External events may heighten or lessen the amplitude of these cycles, but each of these will repeat on their own.

Arthur M. Schlesinger Jr. and his father, Arthur Sr., attributed the internal explanation in political cycles to a shift in emphasis between "public good" and "private interest." He describes times in U.S. history where these periods alternated which I have projected forward to last for about 20 years and 10 years respectively. The over-reach in one period leads to the demands for change in the next. During periods of "public good," government is looked to for solutions to issues of social and economic equality. Investments in the public sector are encouraged. Government has a "social responsibility" that may include regulation of business and protection of civil rights. During periods of "private interest," the emphasis is on less government, a free-market economy, and private property.

Humans at both the individual level and the collective level will grow emotionally exhausted with endless "public action" and the constant idealistic change targeted at the broad spectrum of political issues. Just as the hot weather of the long summer drags on, once welcomed after the rainy, cool spring, people yearn for a cooling-off period that the autumn brings. So too, after an emotional challenge to the status quo, people yearn for a return to the period of "private interest" with more emphasis on free enterprise and less government.

Historian Frank L. Klingberg described how foreign policy moods shifted from "extroversion" (lasting about 27 years) to "introversion"[4] (lasting about 21 years) over a nearly fifty-year cycle in his book *Cyclical Trends in American Foreign Policy Moods* (1983). Klingberg explores the many possible explanations for cycles but emphasizes that the validity of the cycle may well be in the convincing body of evidence of its existence rather than in the causal factors that may or may not be readily isolated. He goes on to define that extroversion is the "willingness to use direct political or military pressure on other nations, while introversion stressed domestic concerns as well as normal economic, humanitarian, and cultural relations abroad."[5]

In specific terms, he defined the years from 1940 to 1967 as a period of extroversion and the years 1967 to 1988 as a period of introversion. It is fair to say that our involvement in WWII, Korea, and Vietnam appear consistent with an extroversion mood. The country, in fact, then completely disengaged from any serious military conflict after Vietnam during the introversion period he described. As his book was published in 1983, a new extroversion phase was expected to span the years from

1989 to 2016. When the Soviet Union collapsed during that time, the U.S. found itself alone as the sole superpower and we quickly broke out of our "introversion" with the first Gulf War in Iraq in 1991, the war in Afghanistan in 2001, and the second Iraq War in 2003. The next introversion phase that Klingberg's theory identified would be expected to run from 2016 to 2037, which would coincide with the coming High period and a renewed, focus on jobs, family, and community. Donald Trump emphasized the need for "America First" in the 2016 Presidential campaign, which suggested a less likely involvement in direct action.

The transformation of the social order in America since 1945 also caught the attention of historian Francis Fukuyama, who chronicled the monumental shifts in American society occurring after 1945 in his fascinating book *The Great Disruption* (1999). While he did not ascribe the causes of these changes directly to cycles, he did point out that that the rise of individualism could give rise to innovation and growth, but also disrupt social norms by challenging authority and weakening families. He remarked optimistically that "social order, once disrupted, tends to get remade again."[6] Hence the same dynamism that disrupts social relations will reshape them.

Generations

William Strauss & Neil Howe have written several books on the many generations that have lived in America. These books serve as a discourse on the history of the country itself, including: *Generations* (1991), *13th Generation* (1993), *The Fourth Turning* (1997) and *Millennials Rising* (2000). They describe a repeating cycle of generational personas that served as the internal explanations for major shifts in society. A generation is described as a group of people born over a period of

(18 – 22) years where their shared experiences create a common identity and persona, acknowledging that differences may exist within the generation in how they view these experiences. Popular musicians for each generation have written songs that capture some part of the generational ethos.

Defiant Baby Boomers in My Generation by The Who, 1965

Cynical Gen X in Smells Like Teen Spirit by Nivirana, 1991

Reluctant Gen Y (Millennials) in Stop This Train by John Mayer, 2006

As each generation reaches a critical stage in their own lives, roughly at age 20, 40, 60 and 80, a shift occurs not only in their lives but in society as a whole. Think of how your own life has changed during any of those important milestones; college, marriage, children, career, or retirement. Each generation sits between two others that have been shaped and influenced by events of their own. Even events that are shared by multiple generations are experienced by them at different stages of their respective lives, and their perspective is viewed through a unique lens. Together, these generations form a collective human chain spanning the lifetime of an individual and covering each of those stages of life: childhood/adolescence, young adult, mid-life, and elderhood. At these critical changes in life stages, each generation enters a new period that demands a fresh resolve for the challenges that each new stage offers and triggers a new "turning" in the collective social order.

Strauss & Howe point to not only common shared experiences which define a generation, but to the broad parenting norms that are applied to them during their childhood and adolescence. Key among these differences are the shifting trends of over- or under-parenting and the effect on the over- or under-protected children. It seems quite natural that children raised with one style may well shift to the other when they become parents. Regardless of the emotional reason for this shift, it serves as an "internal factor" that Schlesinger identified as the reason cycles repeat.

While coming-of-age movies may share a common theme of teenage or young adult emotional growth, the differences between them over the generations reflect the vastly different eras in which the youth grew up. The themes and mood of *The Graduate* are vastly different from those in *The Breakfast Club,* as are the generations that those movies depict. *The Graduate* portrays how a recent college graduate would reject the current norms and eschew a future in "plastics" for a "real" life with the woman he loves. *The Breakfast Club* depicts the lives of four high-school students from different backgrounds, all sharing the same feelings of alienation in the unraveling culture of their time.

The different face of each generation, shaped by the common events they experienced as children, and the parenting style practiced by their parents, results in the values, norms and personality of the generation. Look no further than the mood and attitudes of a high school or college graduation ceremony of one generation compared with those of another. The viewpoint may be more aptly described as how they intend to change the world to reflect their vision, while shifting it from how the generation before them had shaped it.

Mike and the Mechanics echoes how each generation inherits the problems caused by the prior generation in The Living Years released in 1988.

Strauss & Howe explain in their book *Generations* that their theory of generations is a combination of two distinct, but related theories. The first is from the "generation approach" developed by Karl Mannheim, Jose Ortega y Gasset, and others. They term this an "age-location" perspective on history. In effect, this stresses that "events shape the personalities of different age groups differently according to their phase of life"[7] when these key events occur. Consider how 9/11 affected each generation living at that time differently; for Baby Boomers, it was an opportunity to move beyond the Culture Wars of the '90s and provide wise leadership; for Gen X a second chance to find common ground beyond their neglected childhood; and for Millennials the chance to demonstrate their optimism and attitude of teamwork and entrepreneurial spirit.

Their second theory rests on the proposition that generations come in (repeating) cycles of four distinct types. Key among these cycles are two important social events that can be characterized as dominant; a "secular crisis" and a "spiritual awakening." In between these two dominant periods are two recessive transitions that echo or amplify the effects throughout society. These may be positive or negative. For example, after the exhausting period from 1929-1945, where collective action was required to survive, a natural breathing period occurred where people gravitated toward just living life and pursuing families and careers.

Turnings and Archetypes

There are four distinct periods that comprise the generational cycles that affect our society; High,

Awakening, Unraveling, and Crisis. A seasonal metaphor would define these as spring, summer, fall, and winter. When *The Fourth Turning* was first published in 1997, America was deeply in an Unraveling period. Just as the leaves die and fall off trees in the fall, so does the unraveling period see the norms of a prior generation wither along with the trust of institutions that were once venerated. And this fall period invariably leads to the cold winter of a crisis period.

This cycle of four periods coincides with the nearly twenty-year span of a distinct generation to which Strauss & Howe attribute a common persona: Idealists, Reactive, Civic, and Adaptive. During a spiritual Awakening, the Idealists drive the social change through the inner world of values and culture. The Civics respond to the secular Crisis by rebuilding the outer world of institutions. In between these major periods are the "recessive" personas that serve as the glue to society and mitigate or support the actions of their dominant predecessors. Reactives follow Idealists as pragmatists during the Unraveling period and Adaptives follow the Civics as ameliorators during the High.

Intertwined with the generation that is created is a shared "time-location" and the turnings that occur as each generation enters a new phase of life and the society at large enters a new period in the cycle is "a recurring sequence of four generational archetypes"[8] that corresponds to each generation. Strauss and Howe characterize these archetypes as the Prophet, Nomad, Hero, and Artist. These archetypes represent a temperament, or collective persona of each generation.

***The Prophet archetype**, nurtured as indulged children, brings forth an ideal vision of society which they attempt to forge with passion as they come of age. This vision is steeped in spiritual/*

religious values that prioritize the rights of the individual over the established norms of the society as a whole.

***The Nomads**, unprotected as children, grew up indifferent to the bad reputation attributed to them and focus their attention on survival as pragmatic warriors and face problems head on.*

***The Hero (Civic) archetype**, increasingly protected as children, are perceived as good kids and empowered to make their mark on the world. They work together in a cooperative way to focus on building community, gaining influence, and advancing the technologies of their period.*

***The caring Artist archetype**, over-protected as children, appear placid but advance values of pluralism, expertise and due-process. They gravitate toward consensus building and are comfortable with a conformist role.*

Then there are the "turnings," or periods of a new social order made in the image of the generation "coming of age" at the time of the turning.

*"**The First Turning is a High**, an upbeat era of strengthening institutions and weakening individualism, when a new civic order implants and the old values regime decays." [9]*

*"**The Second Turning is an Awakening**, a passionate era of social and spiritual upheaval, when the civic order comes under attack from a new values regime."[10]*

*"**The Third Turning is an Unraveling**, a downbeat era of strengthening individualism and weakening institutions, when the old civic order decays and the new values regime implants."[11]*

*"**The Fourth Turning is a Crisis**, a decisive era secular upheaval, when the values regime propels the replacement of the old civic order with a new one."[12]*

The sequential cadence of these periods gives us a greater perspective of the events that occur during them and the distinct way the generations shape and respond to them. Each period is an essential part of the whole cycle and the accompanying rebirth, growth, maturation and decay of the social order. Each is necessary for the ultimate renewal of society. Judgment of the events as either good or bad should be viewed in this broader context. Just as a fruit tree needs enough chill days during the winter to produce a sweeter fruit, so does a society need the winter cold to chill their social order so it can birth a new one in the spring.

Figure I-4

The Social and Generational Cycle

CRISIS - HERO   HIGH - ARTISTS

UNRAVELING -   AWAKENING -

NOMADS   PROPHETS

The turnings reflect the shift in many of societies' norms around family, child rearing, gender roles, and institutions. As we saw in the last High period, the focus was on strong families, but the trend toward over-protection was loosened as the Silent generation encouraged more freedoms. Trust and faith in institutions of all kinds were strong. There was a focus on doing what works, even if some interest groups were neglected. These also include the shift in focus between the community and the individual captured in the adage, "What's good for the group is good for the individual" or at other times the reverse: "What's good for the individual is good for the group." We will explore these moods in the context of the major political, social and economic events during each turning in the current cycle, along with the persona and impact of the generation coming of age at the time.

Figure I-5

Moods of the Four Turnings				
Social Aspect	First Turning High	Second Turning Awakening	Third Turning Unraveling	Fourth Turning Crisis
Families	strong	weakening	weak	strengthening
Child Rearing	loosening	underprotective	tightening	overprotective
Gender Roles	maximum	narrowing	minimum	widening
Institutions	reinforced	attacked	eroded	founded
Trust in Government	High	Declining	Low	Increasing
Voter Turnout	High	Declining	Low	Increasing
Social Priorities	maximum community	rising individualism	maximum individualism	rising community
New Gen Focus	do what works	fix inner world	do what feels right	fix outer world
Wars	restorative	controversial	inconclusive	decisive

Source: William Strauss and Neil Howe, The Fourth Turning

Figure I-6

Theory of Cycles	1945	1950	1955	1960	1965	1970	1975	1980	1985	1990	1995	2000	2005	2010	2015	2020	2025	2030	2035
Strauss & Howe - Generational Cycles																			
High		High															High		
Awakening						Awakening													
Unraveling										Unraveling									
Crisis												Crisis							
Schlesinger - Political Focus																			
Public Purpose					Public							Public					Public		
Private interest		Private						Private						Private					
Klingberg - Foreign Policy Moods																			
Extrovert		Extrovert										Extrovert							
Introvert							Introvert											Introvert	

Overlapping Cycles

We have examined three different theories of cycles pertaining to political moods (Schlesinger), foreign policy moods (Klingsberg), and generational moods (Strauss & Howe). We will take this a step further by illustrating how all three of these theories may overlap during a common time period and amplify or soften the effects of the others. Human nature and society are complicated phenomena and there may be a variety of forces at work simultaneously, such as these cycles affecting different aspect of society, but working together to produce a unique outcome.

In the last generational High period (Strauss & Howe) starting in 1945, we were also in a period of "private interest" (Schlesinger) and still in an "extroverted" foreign policy mood (Klingberg). It was a golden age for the economy and the free market was unleashed. Standards of living rose markedly. President Truman stood up firmly to unions threatening strikes. But we were also actively involved in remaking the world order after the war. The Marshall plan, the Korean War, the Cuban Missile crisis and the Vietnam War were all "extroverted" foreign policy initiatives. The Silent generation quietly and dutifully went to Korea in the shadow of the larger world war fought by their predecessors, the G.I. Generation (also called The Greatest Generation). So these three different theories of cycles were acting together and simultaneously to shape the events and attitudes of the post-war period.

The Awakening period during the '60s and '70s, with its emphasis on social change, overlapped with an extensive "public good" mood and magnified the cumulative effects throughout the country. Civil-rights issues dominated the period. Government spending on public programs expanded. During that period, we also witnessed a shift from an "extrovert" foreign policy to an "introvert" mood just as the Vietnam War was escalating. The Awakening period amplified the impact of that shift to introversion with vigorous anti-war protests and a military retrenchment after the war ended. A policy of easing of hostilities, "détente," and even the boosting of trade was pursued with Communist China and the Soviet Union in the '70's.

The Unraveling period of the '80s and '90s began with the election of Ronald Reagan as President and his "private interest" policies toward business and government. The economy performed well through most of the '80s after a deep recession in 1981. We were still in an "introvert" foreign policy period then and there was little direct military action of any significance (i.e. Grenada in 1983). The Iran-Contra scandal was a covert action program that went awry. The emphasis was on diplomacy and covert action along with a nuclear arms race. The shift to a nearly thirty-year "extrovert" foreign policy occurred around 1990 and the First Gulf War under President Bush quickly followed. But the collapse of the Soviet Union in 1991 allowed President Clinton to take a more passive approach to foreign policy during his two terms. He was finally forced to act after standing idling by during the atrocities in Bosnia and genocide in Rwanda when Serbia attempted ethnic cleansing in Kosovo. NATO conducted bombings of Serbia until they relented on Kosovo, while Russia, their long-time ally, was unable to respond effectively. The stain on Clinton's legacy from his inaction in Rwanda was far worse than the stain left on the dress of Monica Lewinski. The shift to a "public purpose" political mood occurred during the Clinton administration. But the Republicans quickly took control of Congress and the country endured two government shutdowns. A mixture of legislation benefitting both the public and private good was enacted but major health-care reform was blocked. The Culture Wars of the Unraveling period of the generational

cycle overshadowed the 'public purpose' period of the
political cycle. But a booming economy and the lower
spending from the end of the Cold War nearly eliminated
the government deficit. Meanwhile, the social unraveling
continued.

Our current crisis period began in 2001 during an
"extroverted" foreign policy mood and a "public purpose"
political period. President Bush enacted a major tax cut,
education bill, and Medicare expansion. The lack of
government oversight which led to the financial crisis
and Great Recession of 2007-2008, and the poor response
to Hurricane Katrina were inconsistent with a "public
purpose" mood. A terrorist attack during an "extrovert"
foreign policy mood resulted in the swift reaction to
9/11 in Afghanistan, and the invasion of Iraq quickly
followed. President Obama took a passive approach to
military interventions during the "extrovert" foreign policy
period due to the economic crisis and consistent with his
long-standing ideology. He did ramp up troops levels for a
few years in Afghanistan, but left Iraq quickly and without
a residual presence, and stood aside during the Syria
conflict, even after they crossed his 'red-line' and used
chemical weapons on civilians.

The shift to a "private interest" political mood in 2010,
shortly after Obama took office resulted in the quick shift
in control of Congress to Republican hands -- but six years
of gridlock. The shift from "public purpose" to "private
interest" also coincided with the theme of "America First"
in Trump's campaign in the 2016 Presidential election.
This captured the prevailing mood to focus on economic
development at home and unravel excessive government
regulations. It is also consistent with the start of an
"introverted" foreign policy phase predicted for 2020. It
apparently arrived a few years sooner.

Figure I-7

Theory of Cycles	1945	1950	1955	1960	1965	1970	1975	1980	1985	1990	1995	2000	2005	2010	2015	2020	2025	2030	2035
Strauss & Howe - Generational Cycles																			
High	High															High			
Awakening					Awakening														
Unraveling									Unraveling										
Crisis													Crisis						
Schlesinger - Political Focus																			
Public Purpose				Public					Public							Public			
Private interest	Private						Private						Private						
Klingberg - Foreign Policy Moods																			
Extrovert	Extrovert									Extrovert									
Introvert					Introvert											Introvert			

The upcoming generational High period overlaps with a return to a "public purpose" mood and an "introverted" foreign policy mood. The High period will be a positive time for economic growth, family, and community. But the "public purpose" mood contrasts with the "private interest" mood in the last High period. Perhaps this will result in progress on income inequality as growth in the private sector occurs, along with bi-partisan action on entitlement reform. That may bode well for moderate candidates in the 2020 election. The "introvert" foreign policy mood may help avoid the financial and human cost of war and allow for resources to go elsewhere. The mood would also be consistent with the public aversion for war – because of the false premise that precipitated and the bloody civil war that followed the Iraq War.

Heroes - Good

The alternating role of the Hero and Anti-Hero plays an important part in the persona of the generations and in the turnings themselves. The emergence of comic book Superheroes (Superman) in 1938, as the Great Depression was ending and the threat of world war looming, created a genre which has ebbed and flowed with the social periods since then. Along with Superman came Batman, Captain Marvel, Wonder Woman and Captain America. All possessed extraordinary or even superhuman abilities. At that time, the G.I. generation was coming of age and would personify these heroes in real life. The Silent Generation was in their childhood and these Heroes would have a greater effect on the persona that they were forming.

After WWII ended and the High period began, the impact of superhero comics declined and was replaced with more of a science fiction emphasis, like The Flash and The Green Lantern. This would correspond with the rise of movies during the High period depicting the invasion of Earth by aliens: *The Day the Earth Stood Still* (1951), *The War of the Worlds* (1953), *Invasion of the Body Snatchers* (1956). Heroes in the High period included more human forms like policemen, firefighters, and astronauts as the conventional social norms of the High took hold.

As the country entered the Awakening period, Superhero comics became more political and covered social issues. Even Captain America became disillusioned. The Awakening period also saw the rise of anti-heroes in films such as *Cool Hand Luke, A Clockwork Orange, One Flew Over the Cuckoo's Nest, Dirty Harry* and *The Outlaw Josey Wales.* As the country slipped further into the Unraveling period, the Superhero genre also got darker with *Watchmen* and *The Dark Knight Returns.* Heroes remained in the national psyche and popular culture, but their persona changed with the new generation.

After 9/11, films about Heroes and Superheroes proliferated throughout the current crisis period. There have been over 60 superhero movies released by Marvel and DC comics from when the Crisis period started in 2001 through 2018.[13] Generation Z has spent their entire childhood in the wake of 9/11 and the wars in Afghanistan and Iraq, while being shaped by those superhero movies, as well as by all of the other films honoring real heroes of the wars themselves. Some of the best of these were: *Black Hawk Down* (2001), *The Hurt Locker* (2008), *Green Zone* (2010), *Hell and Back Again* (2011), *Lone Survivor* (2013), and *American Sniper* (2014). Many other war movies during the Crisis period paid homage to the heroes of WWII and Vietnam: the ultimate sacrifices of some to save the one surviving brother of four in *Saving Private Ryan* (1998), the bravery of men of the 101st Airborne in *Band of Brothers* (2001), the valor and loyalty of men in the first major battle between the U.S. soldiers and North Vietnamese regulars in *We Were Soldiers* (2002), the bravery of the enemy facing certain death in *Letters from Iwo Jima* (2006), and the heroic efforts of a conscientious objector who saved lives rather than taking them in *Hacksaw Ridge* (2016).

The collective impact of these films on the overall culture, and the Gen Z youth in particular, has been significant when seen over a span of 15 years or more. In addition, there have been the frequent stories on national and local heroes by the media. The events of each period are reflected back to us in films that also capture the prevailing mood of that period, whether they be hero or anti-hero. Generational memory, like all memory, is created by strong emotional events that occur, and especially if they are repeatedly reinforced on a 50-foot screen with surround sound to young impressionable minds. A hero's ethos has been permanently etched in their psyche.

Villains – Evil

For every hero, there is usually a nemesis. Whether it be an individual like Adolf Hitler or a regime like the Nazi's or an "axis of evil" or "an evil empire," a society will coalesce around a common enemy and their heroes will stand up to those enemies. Over the course of history, the enemy of one nation has usually been another country, with identifiable leaders and borders. The use of terrorism to murder civilians and create fear among society is an important element of this story and the "terrorist' is one of the central antagonists of the crisis period. A brief discussion of its evolution is worthwhile.

Terrorism, as we know it today, became a strategy of warfare by members of a weaker populace against the stronger ruling class in the 20th century as nationalists strove to combat colonial rule in many parts of the world. The Kurdistan Workers Party (PKK), formed in the 1970s, used terrorist tactics to announce its goal of a Kurdish state in their historical homeland in southeastern Turkey. The Irish Republican Army (IRA) resorted to terrorism as part of their aim to create an independent state apart from the United Kingdom. After the Bloody Sunday massacre of thirteen civilians during a protest march in Derry, Northern Ireland, in 1972, the IRA quickly responded with the detonations of 20 bombs in Belfast, killing thirteen innocents, in what became known as Bloody Friday. The Palestinian Black September group took eleven Israeli Olympic athletes hostage at the Munich Olympics in 1972 and eventually killed them in a quest to release several hundred Palestinian prisoners being held in Israeli prisons.

During the years of America's "counter-culture" movement, student protests gave way to violent attacks by the Weather Underground, frustrated by the lack of progress with peaceful protests, on government buildings and banks. On October 6, 1969, the Weathermen blew up the statue of a Chicago policeman with arm raised high, erected in Chicago to commemorate the seven policemen who died during the Haymarket labor riots in 1886. The Weathermen may have chosen this symbolic target as the Haymarket Riots coincided with the start of the last Awakening period in America eighty (80) years earlier. Other home-grown terrorists mimicked Timothy McVeigh, who struck at a government building in Oklahoma City in 1995 and killed innocent civilians as well as their children being cared for in the day-care facility where their mothers worked.

But in 2001, terrorists from the al-Qaeda group in the Middle East hijacked our planes and killed thousands of our men and women here in America. The plan was directed from Afghanistan, became synonymous with Osama bin Laden and the conservative Taliban who were harboring him. America was again going to a distant, unfamiliar land, not to prevent the fall of dominos, but to defeat an enemy that had attacked the homeland. The "war on terror" would dominate the language of our news media and politicians throughout the crisis period. America had a new villain, terrorists or an axis of evil that resembled them.

Recent Turnings in America

To provide a better understanding of the cycle of social and generational change in America, we will briefly explore the most recent four 'turnings' in our history since the end of World War II. Let's take an overview of the most recent High, Awakening, Unraveling, and Crisis periods before we conduct a more in-depth look at each one in later chapters. Each period, for better or worse, is a necessary part of the cycle.

1. High Period

The last crisis period spanned the sixteen years from 1929 to 1945 and included the Great Depression, the Dust Bowl, the attack on Pearl Harbor, and WWII. President Truman took over after FDR died and brought the war to a victorious end after dropping the atomic bomb on Hiroshima and Nagasaki. After the Japanese surrendered, the country was ready for peace, stability, and prosperity. A new High period was born and millions of soldiers returned home. The economy boomed and created enough jobs to keep unemployment relatively low, while the G.I. Bill provided financial aid for many veterans to go to college to get a better education. This particular High period would also be known as "The American High," as American economic and military power rose to global dominance.

The High period ran from 1945 until 1963, during which the focus was on jobs, family, and community. The American Dream was available to many and consumerism became part of our way of life. This was in sharp contrast to the frugal scrimping and overall lack that marked the Great Depression in the previous crisis period. Gross Domestic Product was strong throughout much of the High period and has been viewed nostalgically, as average GDP growth was progressively lower in subsequent periods.

Figure I-8

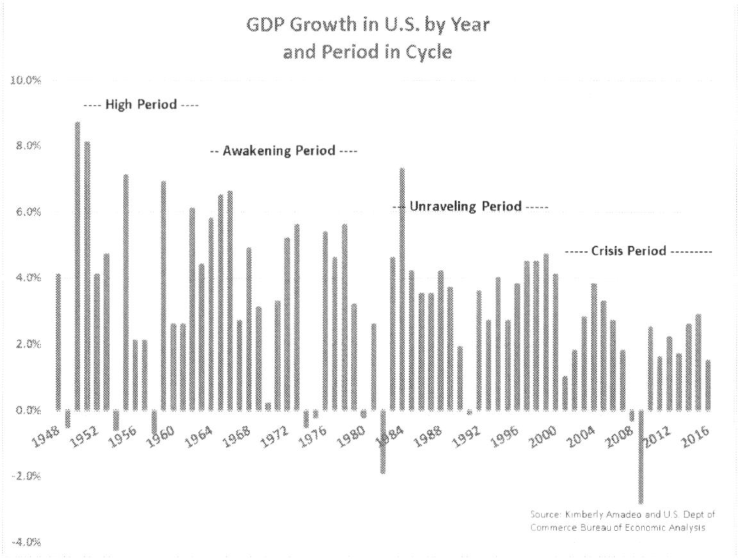

GDP Growth in U.S. by Year and Period in Cycle

Source: Kimberly Amadeo and U.S. Dept of Commerce Bureau of Economic Analysis

Truman implemented the Marshall Plan to rebuild democracies in Europe. Communism was the new enemy that had spread from Russia to Eastern Europe, which was tightly locked behind an Iron Curtain. China would fall to the Communists in 1949 and we would fight to a stalemate to contain it in Korea. The search for Communists spread to the homeland where Congress investigated citizens to determine their allegiance. Although Truman faced many labor disputes, social conformity was the norm. The Silent generation was largely content to enjoy the comforts of the new materialism and conform to the status quo. Currents of social dissent were visible, but would not boil over until the next period.

The truculent and unpopular Truman gave way to a likeable "Ike," war hero and grandfather. Highways were built that connected and expanded America across the continent. The country prospered and a new generation was born in record numbers. Women tended to the home while the men filled jobs in the offices and factories of America. New technologies brought televisions and appliances to American homes, increasingly built in the suburbs. Gender roles widened and took on a traditional feel that reminded many of the good ole days.

A young, vibrant, progressive was elected President in 1960 and the optimistic mood of the High period began to feel like a new Camelot. The Cold War was in full swing and President Kennedy would be embroiled in a nuclear chess match with the Soviet Union, after a failed attempt to overthrow the Communist regime in Cuba. Trust in government was high and America was a superpower. But The High period was losing steam, and many unresolved social issues were clearly visible below the surface. The High period ended with the sounds of rifle shots from the 6th floor of the Dallas Book Depository on November 22, 1963.

2. Awakening Period

The mood of the country changed decidedly on that day and the Awakening period had begun. The country would be shaken from the stability it had enjoyed since VJ Day (Victory in Japan) with the social, political and cultural events of the ensuing seventeen years. President Johnson was quickly sworn in as the next President while on Air Force One standing next to a dazed Jacqueline Kennedy, still in the bloodied pink Chanel suit she wore while sitting next to her husband when he was shot. His sudden and tragic death immediately changed the mood of the country. Suspicions of a conspiracy and CIA involvement began to erode public confidence. The sudden shift in mood tore away the façade of conformity and revealed the simmering dissatisfaction of women, blacks, and young people.

The High period had given way to a new Awakening period, which would extend from 1963 to 1980. The Awakening period upended many of the norms and values that had set in during the American High. The new Baby Boomer generation came of age and challenged all the social norms and created new ones that reflected their ideals. The Baby Boomers had enjoyed many conveniences as children that their grandparents and parents could only dream of. High school graduation rates had swelled from 40% in 1940 to nearly 70% by 1960. The new generation went off to college at higher rates than before. The universities across America would serve as a breeding ground for a new phenomenon – student activism and social protest.

The Vietnam War would deeply divide the country and over 58,000 young men would lose their lives. Returning veterans would not receive parades and adulation like generations before them, but scorn for the unpopular government policy they served to implement. Like

Truman, Johnson would only serve one term beyond the one he inherited from a dead president; both leaders were the casualties of unsuccessful wars. Trust in government dropped steadily throughout the Awakening period while crime rose rapidly.

The Awakening period unleashed the ground swell of discontent that had been building during the High period. Women now had access to the birth-control pill and birth rates plummeted, while divorce rates soared. The sexual revolution would sweep across America. The women's movement pressed for an equal-rights amendment, but the status quo pushed back. An environmental movement was born out of Rachel Carson's book *Silent Spring* (1962), which resulted in the banning of DDT and the subsequent creation of the EPA. Organic farms and food businesses were started by young entrepreneurs as an expression of their personal beliefs and mission, never imagining how mainstream organic foods would become today.

Women received another victory when the Supreme Court ruled in favor of a woman's right to an abortion in 1973. But the country was deeply divided on this issue. Those who favored the conservative status quo of the High period did not agree with the progressive changes of the Awakening period. They fought to keep the values and norms they believed it. But abortion was now a woman's right and was legal in all 50 states. Abortions rose dramatically from 1973 until they peaked in 1980, with the greater availability and use of birth control.

Blacks had secured some progress on civil rights during the High period, but patience had grown thin with the unavoidable reality of pervasive discrimination and poverty. Violence marred the peaceful march from Selma to Montgomery, but television made the plight of the blacks real to everyone. The Civil Rights Act of 1964 and the Voting Rights Act of 1965 helped to bring about some structural change, but ended the long standing Democratic voting bloc in the South. The blighted urban areas were set ablaze when Martin Luther King Jr. was assassinated.

Just as television transformed the country as a new visual medium, so did music as a medium for political dissent with the musician as the orator. Folk singer Bob Dylan gave poetic voice to the causes of the civil rights and anti-war movements. Rock 'n roll would soon amplify that message even louder with the electric guitar. Drugs, long-hair, and concerts would personify the peace movement as well as the new generation. The Summer of Love in 1967 would start with a peaceful concert in Monterey and performances by established and new musicians who would all become legendary.

The Awakening period would become known for the assassination of progressive figures, with JFK being the first. When the networks announced, "We interrupt this program to bring you a special announcement," our hearts paused as we knew it was not just another "breaking news" story. So when the non-violent Martin Luther King, Jr. was murdered in April of 1968, we feared the response would be emotional, and violence ensued as blacks in poor urban areas rioted in anger and frustration. When President Johnson declined to run for re-election in the 1968 Presidential race, the door was opened for Robert Kennedy to succeed his murdered brother. After an essential victory in the California primary, Bobby was assassinated in the kitchen of the Ambassador hotel in Los Angeles. The emotional appeal and popularity of Bobby was missing when Hubert Humphrey lost to Richard Nixon in the anti-climactic presidential election later that year.

The economy also experienced turmoil throughout the Awakening period. The deficits created by the unfunded war in Vietnam resulted in rising inflation in the late '60s. The economy suffered an oil shock in the early '70s that disrupted the comfortable consumer society everyone had come accustomed to. OPEC implemented production cuts and imposed an embargo on the U.S. in 1973 in retaliation for the U.S. support of Israel during their Yom Kippur War with Arab states. Inflation soared to nearly 12% and unemployment to 9% by 1975. Conflict in the Middle East had now affected the economic stability of the homeland. Long gas lines frustrated our love affair with our cars and the freedom they symbolized. The geo-political importance of the oil-rich Middle East became apparent to everyone in America and an era of military intervention there by the U.S. was born.

The turmoil of the period flooded into the political arena with the break-in of the DNC HQ in the Watergate hotel in 1972. The subsequent investigation revealed a cover-up by the Nixon administration. Events culminated in his resignation after articles of impeachment were drawn up for a vote in the House. He was subsequently pardoned by his successor, President Ford. But this paved the way for an unknown Democratic peanut farmer from Georgia to be elected President in 1976.

The Awakening period is, by its nature, an exhausting time of social change. By the late '70s that energy was running its course. President Carter faced another energy shock in 1979 when the Iranian revolution resulted in significant oil-production cuts in that country, causing inflation to rise to 14% by 1980. To make matters worse, the capture of the hostages at the American embassy in Tehran would be more than the Carter presidency could endure. Carter lost to Ronald Reagan in a landslide in the 1980 Presidential election, who won on a campaign slogan of "Let's Make America Great Again." The Awakening period was over.

3. Unraveling Period

America had now entered the next phase of the cycle, the Unraveling period, which would run from 1980 to 2001. The conflict between those who championed the changes of the Awakening period and those who preferred the status quo values of the prior High period would come to a head in a protracted culture war throughout the period. The Unraveling period coincided with the coming of age of Gen X. They grew up as the unprotected children during the Awakening when their parents were likely to get divorced. Gen X had been raised to survive on their own and this persona carried over into their young adult period. They were not very concerned what society thought of them, as they did not care much for a society that had abandoned them. This persona carried over to their music, attire, and attitude. The movie *The Breakfast Club* captured the common angst of an eclectic cross-spectrum of Gen X teenagers.

Unraveling periods start out with brief improvement in the mood, but then it invariably slides into a full-blown unraveling of the social order. National unity was at a fever pitch after the U.S. Olympic hockey team defeated the superior Soviet team in the semi-finals in 1980. After a failed attempt at the Republican National Convention in 1976 to displace the sitting President Ford from the nomination, Ronald Reagan succeeded in taking control of the party and won the Presidency in 1980, in a landslide against a beleaguered and politically sapped President Carter.

The mood shifted and seemed that it might decidedly improve again with the "Let's Make America Great Again" campaign slogan. As Ronald Reagan was being sworn in as President on January 20, 1981, the hostages in Iran were being freed after 444 days in captivity. Americans were enthralled months later when Prince Charles and Lady Diana were married. But it was a short-lived optimism. The Culture Wars over social issues had begun and the two sides were committed to battle fiercely for their causes. Economic and foreign policy issues also divided the nation. Then a deep recession struck in 1982 and unemployment rose to nearly 11% by November of 1982. Deregulation, globalization, and corporate restructuring would help boost corporate profits, but stagnate incomes for the middle class. America became aware that a virus was infecting and killing many homosexual men. HIV and AIDS became a worldwide concern. Crime, abortion, and divorce would all peak in 1980, but the damage done to the social fabric would affect the entire Unraveling period.

Bruce Springsteen vividly describes the pain suffered by people dying of AIDS in his haunting 1993 song, Streets of Philadelphia, which also served as the soundtrack for the movie, Philadelphia (aka The City of Brotherly Love).

President Reagan would go on to win a second landslide victory against Walter Mondale, but his legacy was tarnished by the Iran-Contra scandal where arms were sold to the Contras in Nicaragua (in violation of Congressional legislation). He would be revered by future Republicans as the consummate conservative, yet his large tax cuts and increased defense spending drove deep budget deficits. His folksy style and ardent patriotism gave him the ability to connect with most Americans at a time when they sorely needed positive leadership after the tumultuous Awakening period. Yet trust in government hovered between only 40% and 50% during his presidency and voter turnout was only 53% for both of his victories.

The risk of nuclear war between the Soviet Union and the U.S. weighed on people's minds as the arms race escalated and there were enough nukes to destroy the planet many times over. The movie *The Day After* premiered in 1983 and captured the attention of 100 million people in the country. The fearful mood was palpable. Even nuclear power didn't feel safe after meltdowns at Three Mile Island in 1979 and Chernobyl in 1986. The explosion of the Space Shuttle Challenger shortly after take-off in 1986 only added to the uncertainty of man's command of technology.

Foreign affairs took a turn for the better when Mikhail Gorbachev became Secretary General of the Communist Party of the Soviet Union in 1985 following the deaths of Brezhnev, Andropov, and Chernenko in quick succession. An arms reduction treaty was negotiated with the U.S. and the Berlin Wall was torn down by citizens of both East and West Germany in 1989. One after the other, communist countries in Eastern Europe broke away from the Soviet Union and were free to experiment with democracy. East and West Germany were united in 1990 after 45 years of control by the Soviet Union.

The United States held a strong position on the global stage when Iraq invaded Kuwait in 1990. President Bush quickly organized a broad coalition of countries to support Operation Desert Storm in 1990 and had the support of the American electorate as well. Iraq was quickly pushed out of Kuwait and coalition forces pursued them toward Bagdad. But President Bush stopped short of entering Baghdad and toppling Saddam Hussein on the advice of many of who warned that a sectarian war would ensue. But some troops were left in Saudi Arabia, the location of Muslim holy sites in Medina and Meccas, which would come to be a motivating flashpoint for al-Qaeda's war against the U.S.

Trust levels in government would spike upward after the war during the mid-point in President Bush's presidency. Bush had hoped that the successful war in Iraq and the collapse of the Soviet Union would carry him to victory. But he lost a chance for a second term when the economy dipped into recession and unemployment rose to nearly 8% in the months before the 1992 election. "It's the economy stupid" and Bush's fateful "read my lips, no new taxes" pledge were perhaps the simplest explanation for his loss. President Bush lost decisively to Bill Clinton, but Ross Perot, who ran as a third-party candidate, garnered 19 million votes. It is still debatable whether Perot actually cost Bush the election, as Clinton won 370 electoral votes to only 168 for Bush and most of Perot's votes were in states that Bush and Clinton won as expected. The NAFTA agreement was approved by the Congress and President Clinton in 1993 and went into effect the following year. Trade would soar but the loss of traditional jobs of many in the U.S. would accelerate with globalization.

The Democrats quickly lost control of the Congress in the 1994 mid-term elections and a government shutdown over spending soon followed in 1995-96. Clinton's lies about his sexual indiscretions with an intern would drag himself and the country through another impeachment proceeding which lowered the cultural bar even further. The country was in for many more years of political polarization after that. The bright spot was that the economy boomed in the '90s while military spending dropped with the end of the Cold War, eliminating the budget deficits prevalent in the '80s. Inflation and unemployment trended down, the stock market soared and trust in government rose steadily. The '90s began to look like the Roaring '20s with rising wealth and income for many.

The Unraveling period would be a time of radical change in technology. The invention of the personal computer and subsequent development of the World Wide Web and the internet would revolutionize the business world and the personal lives of nearly everyone on the planet. More sophisticated software applications would be developed for large computers and personal ones that would drive productivity gains. Hand-held cell phones would be developed in the '90s that would begin to change the way of life for everyone. Smart phones were not far off.

But something was amiss within the social fabric. The unraveling of the American social culture continued. As we moved into the '90s the Cold War was replaced with the Culture Wars between Americans themselves. Progressives and Conservatives battled over abortion, crime, education, religion, and the role of government in these issues and many more. Then in 1999, the unthinkable happened. Two deranged students massacred 12 students and a teacher at Columbine high school in Colorado. The murders were seared into the minds of the young generation coming of age soon – the Millennials, or Gen Y.

The advent of cable television in the 1980s had a significant effect on the social norms of the country. We became inundated with 24/7 news, which quickly turned into a profit center, with serious journalism suffering. Cable networks turned to salacious programming such as Morton Downey Jr, Geraldo Rivera, and Jerry Springer to boost ratings. Americans tuned in and the cultural bar again dropped lower. The middle class was losing ground economically and socially. Cable programming shifted to reality television in the '90s with the advent of *Real World* and *Road Rules*. This would later give rise to *Big Brother* and *Survivor*, which Gen X could personally relate to, having survived on their own wits as children during the '60s and '70s. As the new millennium and fears about Y2K approached, the Unraveling period was coming to a close. Many people were doing well financially, the Cold War was over, and material well-being appeared good, but the country was torn on the inside, politically and socially.

And a new threat was emerging from those without a nation-state of their own, possessing a radical, religious ideology and a hated for the infidel's presence in their region. Terrorists. Without the means of fighting wars in the conventional manner, they turned their enemy's own resources against them.

4. Crisis Period

The mood of the country shifted suddenly and dramatically on the morning of September 11, 2001, when several planes were hijacked and crashed into the World Trade Center, the Pentagon and a grassy field in southwestern Pennsylvania, killing 2,996 and injuring over 6,000 people. Since the attacks were spread out over several hours, most Americans watched the plane slam into the second tower and explode on live television. Soon after, both towers imploded, taking many more to a smoldering grave of concrete and steel. I stared in disbelief as the towers fell. We were all stunned by the images in front of us.

From that moment, and for some time thereafter, we all felt a sense of unity around who we were as a people and what we stood for as a nation. That shared pain bound us together after nearly 40 years of divisive political and social conflict. Once again, our homeland had been suddenly attacked and the collective response was the same. We would join together as Americans to fight and defeat a reviled enemy in a distant land. This common cause was felt even between strangers when their eyes met on the subway, in a coffee shop, or on the streets of America, as their heads would nod in agreement with a solemn but determined grimace. The sentiment was captured in the words "United We Stand" that were emblazed on bumper stickers and on placards in windows throughout the homeland. Police, firefighters, and first responders were our heroes again, along with the selfless passengers who forced United Airlines Flight 93 into the ground rather than have it used to kill others. Trust in government soared to levels not seen in over thirty years as we embarked on a just and noble war against the perpetrators of this heinous act. Global compassion for our losses and support for our just cause reinforced our sense of national unity.

Although the general public may not have fully realized it, the U.S. conducted this war with a very limited footprint of boots on the ground. The CIA and Special Forces worked with the regional warlords around Afghanistan, like the Northern Alliance, who had been marginalized when the Taliban took control of the government in Kabul in 1996. The combined efforts of the U.S. forces on the ground and Air Force strikes from above coordinated with the well-armed militia, resulted in a swift defeat of the Taliban in 2002. Unfortunately, when the Taliban regrouped and launched an insurgency in 2003, the U.S. had already moved on to another war of its own making in Iraq.

We invaded Iraq based on false intelligence that Saddam Hussein held vast reserves of weapons of mass destruction (WMD's). We quickly achieved our military objectives, but the political solution proved elusive and Iraq plunged into civil war between the two main religious groups. President Bush's approval rating and trust in government plunged with it. The opportunity to bind the U.S. together during a crisis slipped away with each roadside IED and American casualty. The partisan political divide at home widened again. The public mood worsened.

The eye of Hurricane Katrina slammed into the Gulf coast in 2005 and the government's ineptitude in its aftermath only made matters worse. The housing bubble burst in 2007 and quickly bankrupted Lehman Brothers. The economy was on the verge of collapse and required the financial rescue (bailout) of Merrill Lynch, AIG, Freddie Mac and Fannie Mae. Unemployment soared to 10% and millions of people lost their homes or saw their equity evaporate. The country was in a full-blown economic crisis and fighting two wars in the Middle East. America had entered a crisis period on September 11, 2001, just as we had on October 30, 1929, when the stock market crashed. That earlier crisis period would continue for sixteen years and claim the lives of tens of millions of people worldwide. This new crisis period would not be as severe as the last, but would affect the mood and culture of the country in a similar way. And just as we survived that crisis period and entered a new High period of stability, growth, and community, so will we survive this one and begin a period of American renewal.

So, let's begin a more in-depth exploration of the major social, political, economic, and foreign-policy events that marked these four periods and the generations that came-of-age during them. We shall examine how women and minorities fared in these periods and how political and economic events shaped and amplified the mood. Most importantly, we shall weigh the impact that each new generation had on the period, and how their youthful energy imbued the country with a new ethos. We will begin with the last High period and survey the generational moods and attitudes that prevailed, keeping in mind how these might assert themselves in the upcoming High period.

Chapter 1
America's Last High Period (1945 – 1963)

"The First Turning is a High, an upbeat era
of strengthening institutions and weakening
individualism, when a new civic order implants and
the old values regime decays."[14]

The High period manifests itself in a broad range of
social behaviors and attitudes: families are strong and
child-rearing loosens as the crisis has ended, the gap in
gender roles is at a maximum yet each has a distinctive but
important role, trust in government and voter turnout is
high as optimism about the future prevails, the priority is
on doing what works and rebuilding a sense of community,
wars are few and less severe and tend toward restoring
pre-crisis status or closing unresolved issues.

Figure 1-1

Turning	Period	Families	Child Rearing	Gap in Gender Roles	Trust in Government	Voter Turnout	Social Priorities	New Gen Focus	Wars
First Turning	High	Strong	Loosening	Maximum	High	High	Max Community	do what works	restorative

The most recent First Turning in America ran from the
end of WWII to the assassination of President Kennedy.
This period of time has also been referred to as the
American High by William L. O'Neill in his book of
the same title and *The Best Years: 1945-1950* by Joseph
Goulden in his book on a slice of that period. These
eighteen years were a period of rapid economic growth
that radically raised the standard of living for millions of
Americans. This period in American history started out
with radio addresses by FDR and ended with America

wired for television from coast to coast, which more affluent Americans viewed in color.

The "turning" from the Crisis period to the new High period was marked with finality by the unconditional surrender of the Japanese aboard the USS Missouri on August 14, 1945. The suffering and upheaval in the lives of so many Americans from the stock market crash on October 30, 1929 and resulting Great Depression, through the Japanese attack on Pearl Harbor and the war in Europe and Asia, finally came to an end with D-Day and victory in Europe, and the dropping of the atomic bombs on Japan and Victory in Japan (VJ Day). Tens of millions had died worldwide in the conflict – a staggering amount fortunately not seen in any war since then.

A new mood was ushered in, best exemplified by the famous photo of the swooning kiss between a sailor and a young woman in Times Square. Films in 1946 were quick to capture the new sentiment in *"It's a Wonderful Life"* and *"The Best Years of Our Lives."* The Silent Generation was turning twenty and would take their place behind the "Greatest Generation", who were returning from war and would be taking new roles as the captains of industry, politicians in government, and workers in the exploding middle class in America. Saving the country and the world would be a tough act to follow for the generation coming of age at the end of the war, but they had been raised to follow suit. They earned the name "The Silent Generation" because they appeared to have exchanged a comfortable standard of living for (silent) acceptance of the status quo. The Silent Generation defined the High period, but it also corresponds to the birth and childhood of the Baby Boomer generation.

Figure 1-2

	Order Period - 1945 - 1963			
	Children	Young Adults	Mid-Life Adults	Elders
Generation	Baby Boomers	Silent	G.I.	Lost
Archetype	Prophet	Artist	Hero	Nomad

The caring Artist archetype, over-protected as children, appear placid but advance values of pluralism, expertise and due-process. They gravitate toward consensus-building and are comfortable with a conformist role.

As construction of low-cost new homes soared, Americans moved out of their stacked existence in cities and into more spacious, individual homes in what became known as the suburbs. Innovation and mass production, perfected during the war to make airplanes, tanks, and other weapons, shifted to making automobiles, appliances, and furniture, while rising income levels allowed many families to buy these and other conveniences.

While the country flourished in many tangible ways, it lagged in many other ways. Women returned to the homes from the factories as men replaced them as they returned from war. Racial prejudices were rampant, and children raised during the crisis period were well-behaved, but raised to conform. But strengthening institutions, a growing economy, and a stable social regime were the priorities after nearly twenty years of turmoil and sacrifice. And trust in government was at high levels when Pew Research first began tracking it in 1958.

Figure 1-3 Trust in Government

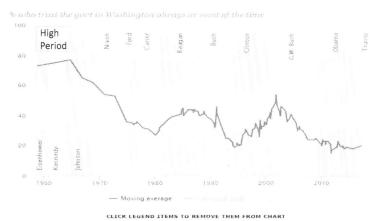

% who trust the gov't in Washington always or most of the time

PEW RESEARCH CENTER

Portrait of the Silent Generation

America had turned the corner from the largely agrarian 19th century to the industrialization of the 20th century and raced past World War I into the Roaring '20s. A new generation was born as the crisis era began with the Great Depression and continued with World War II. Birth rates declined with the austerity of the times. Their elders would go off to fight in the war to save democracy in Europe and stop Japanese imperialism in Asia, while others grew up at home and did what they could to help with the war effort. They had "the lowest rates for almost every social pathology of youth (crime, suicide, illegitimate births, and teen unemployment)."[15] When their time came to serve in Korea, it was to a sanguine and bloody stalemate. They would be appreciated, unlike the Vietnam veterans, but would not receive the ticker-tape parades like those of the victorious G.I. Generation.

They were dutiful and humble but in the context of generational cycles, they served a vital ameliorating purpose to transition between the costly Crisis period and the turbulent Awakening period. Joseph Goulden spoke of an America that "went into a holding period – intellectually, morally, and politically"[16] in the 1950's. He added that the "pause was inevitable, even necessary; the nation was weary."[17] As the generation came of age they stepped forward 'silently' to fulfill their purpose and place in society. They prospered as young adults during the economic expansion of the post-war period. They married early, had babies, and moved to the suburbs.

As they aged into mid-life during the Awakening period of the '60s, the Silent generation split allegiance on cultural issues, with some aligning with the status quo and the G.I. generation and others finding new purpose with the youthful rebellion of the Baby Boomers. Some of the Silent enthusiastically joined the anti-war protests (Daniel Ellsberg and Abbie Hoffman) and women's movement (Gloria Steinem), while others became leaders of the diverse civil-rights movement (Martin Luther King, Jr., Malcolm X, Caesar Chavez, and Russell Means). They had witnessed how these issues were minimized during their youth and sought to resolve them during their adult life. Many of the Silent generation joined the sexual revolution as well and divorce rates soared to new highs.

Yet not a single member of the Silent generation has become President. They have watched from the sidelines as Presidents were chosen from the G.I. Generation (Kennedy, Johnson, Nixon, Ford, Carter, Reagan, and Bush) and then they were skipped over as successive Baby Boomers (Clinton, Bush, Obama, and Trump) rose to prominence. Their disappointment was punctuated by the assassination of two of their generation's greatest leaders; Robert Kennedy and Martin Luther King, Jr. They would make their mark in government with the first women Justice on the Supreme Court in Sandra Day O'Connor.

Women and Family

Women were displaced from the jobs they heroically and capably filled during the war to make room for the millions of men returning from Europe and Asia. The expectations and norms of the times required most of them to become stay-at-home wives and moms, even if some may have harbored personal ambitions and dreams for more. The women's baseball league, which was created to entertain people at home while keeping an American tradition alive during the war, was disbanded after the war, as depicted in Tom Hank's film *A League of their Own (1992)*. Women were now expected to fill their role back at home and help to birth a new generation of Americans who would come to be called Baby Boomers. The new homes in the suburbs along with the new conveniences such as cars, televisions, and appliances would mark a new era in American culture. William L. O'Neill remarked in his book, *American High*, that "members of the generation wanted to go back...to a time of secure values and traditional practices"[18] It was a time for success, comfort and conformity.

Births soared as soldiers returned from the war, married, and began to have families. Baby Boomers were being born. The rapid increase in births strained the education system, as many teachers changed professions after the war, and additional classrooms were needed. Women skipped college, married younger, and had more children than their mothers. A 1962 Gallup Poll of 2,300 women published in *The Saturday Evening Post* showed cracks in the social order being developed, as 90% of women did not wish their daughters to follow in their footsteps and would pursue an education. But many women, usually older and from the middle class, still held jobs outside the home. With the economy growing quickly, there was a shortage of teachers and clerical help. But "feminism" was virtually non-existent.

Figure 1-4.

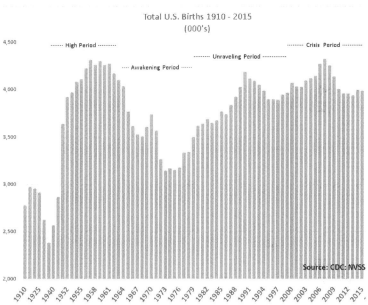

The rate of divorce in the High period was low (below 10%) and frowned upon social and morally. Abortion was illegal but still occurred, and the risks to a woman's life were high. Although sexual roles and norms were considered conservative during the High period, The Kinsey Reports on sexuality (Male 1948 and Female 1953) and Masters and Johnson studies on human sexual response challenged conventional thinking on sexuality and laid the groundwork for the sexual revolution in the Awakening period in the 1960s. Many expressed moral outrage at the time, especially on the report on the sexual behavior (and desires) of women – who were expected to be just nurturing mothers without overt sexual needs of their own.

Pop Culture

The post-war High period was undoubtedly one of the greatest periods of economic advancement in history. People's lives and welfare were transformed. While progress in "private matters" held center-stage and much was accomplished, the euphoria, conformity and stability masked a sub-culture of unresolved issues beneath the surface. This dichotomy was visible in the world of art, literature and music. Voice was given to some of these themes by writers such as J.D. Salinger in *Catcher in the Rye* (1951) and Jack Kerouac's *On the Road* (1957). Hollywood echoed this underlying discontent with films such as *The Wild Ones* (1954) and *Rebel Without A Cause* (1955).

Television and the advent of mass media would rise in tandem with the new life in suburbia. Jackie Gleason achieved fame with his family sit-com *The Honeymooners*. The new mood in America was modeled and personified in the family-oriented television shows like *Father Knows Best, Leave it To Beaver,* and *I Love Lucy*. The widened gender roles were clearly visible and the expected roles for men, women, and children to play were scripted for a High period when people were understandably searching for normalcy and stability.

Several conventional genres dominated the screen in the '50s; romance, westerns, and suspense among others. Although he started making films in the late '20s, Alfred Hitchcock's classic suspense films in this period captivated the audiences: *Spellbound, Rear Window, North by Northwest, Dial M for Murder* and *Vertigo*. Romance and sexuality in film was given a new look with Marilyn Monroe in *Seven Year Itch, Some Like It Hot,* and *The Asphalt Jungle*, while Audrey Hepburn played more traditional female roles in *Sabrina, Roman Holiday,* and *Breakfast at Tiffany's*. Westerns recalled the not so distant past in America history in classics such as *The Searchers, High Noon, Shane, and Rio Bravo* and reinforced traditional values. The real-life fear of global war with the Soviets was replaced with a more imagined-fear of attack by aliens in *The Day the Earth Stood Still, Invasion of the Body Snatchers, War of the Worlds, The Thing from Another World,* and more.

The world of music would undergo change, like the rest of American culture, in the 1950s. Big bands had already given way to pop and crooners like Bing Crosby and Frank Sinatra. Jazz continued to evolve from the big band format of the 1920s and '30s as Duke Ellington and Thelonious Monk took the stage. Rock n' roll music would emerge as a powerful new genre which challenged the musical status quo. Les Paul invented the electric guitar in the '40s, paving the way for musicians to add a new dimension to their vocals. The music of the High period can best be characterized as 'before Elvis' and 'after' Elvis. In January, 1956, Elvis Presley released his hit album and the single "Heartbreak Hotel" shortly after. Elvis challenged the existing clean-cut norms with overt sexual appeal through his unique blend of gospel, R&B, and country. While the FCC censors could control content on television and radio, musicians like Presley could reach people in live venues and created a frenzy among young women long before the Beatles had ever formed a band.

Rock n' roll also gave greater visibility to black performers such Chuck Berry, Little Richard, and Bo Diddley, but the majority of blacks were relegated to limited exposure due to the overt racial prejudices prevalent at that time. The foundation for the musical revolution in the '60s was being laid and performers such as Carl Perkins, Muddy Waters, Howlin' Wolf, and Buddy Holly would be a major influence on the music of The Beatles and The Rolling Stones.

Country music ranged from the traditional with Hank Williams and Patsy Cline of the Nashville sound and rockabilly, with Bill Haley and Elvis Presley, who merged country and rock n' roll. As the '50s continued, a folk revival emerged with performers such as Pete Seeger, the Kingston Trio, and Woody Guthrie. This would the form the basis for using music to protest and give voice to issues affecting society.

But during any period, the prevailing mood overpowers dissenting voices, whether they be for reform or for the status quo. This was the time for those who would conform to the status quo, not rebel against it.

Civil Rights

At the time that whites were moving to the suburbs, blacks and other minorities were replacing them in the inner cities in growing numbers. While whites commuted into the cities for their jobs, the minorities were working in the cities at lower-paying jobs, commensurate with their lack of formal skills and education. This growing concentration of poor, uneducated blacks in the cities, along with the prevailing racial prejudices against them, would remain one of the unresolved issues of the American High until exploding during the Awakening period. The seeds of conflict in one period of the cycle are planted in the ground of neglected issues in another.

Poverty still affected nearly one-third of the country, especially minorities who did not gain as much as others during the period of economic growth. The Civil Rights

Movement gained traction with the 1954 Supreme Court decision in Brown v. Board of Education which held segregation unconstitutional. The case was argued by Thurgood Marshall, an attorney for the National Association for the Advancement of Colored People (NAACP), who would later be appointed to the Supreme Court. Tensions rose quickly with the stand-off at Little Rock's Central High School in 1957, where moderate Republican President Eisenhower sent in federal troops to enforce desegregation. Television brought the images into everyone's home and affected public opinion, as it would for decades to come.

The plight of blacks in the South was hard to ignore with the new visual medium, even within the comforts of one's own home. The arrest of Rosa Parks in 1955 for refusing to give up her seat on the bus to a white person after a long day at work resonated with many people, regardless of color, who could relate to her plight. These acts of civil disobedience and growing support in the Democratic-controlled Congress culminated in the passage of the Civil Rights Act of 1957, forbidding attempts to intimidate blacks from voting. Following its passage, the southern states would soon no longer be the reliable Democratic voting block they had been for decades. They would vote decidedly for Republicans or conservative Independents. Women's rights, civil rights, and environmental issues were already present and simmering to anyone who would look more closely. But the comfortable mood for the status quo was firmly entrenched and could rely on the inertia of a disinterested public to remain dormant for a few years more.

Economy

The economy had quickly shifted from producing weapons and armaments to producing consumer goods and industrial goods for business. An immediate challenge was a lack of housing for the returning soldiers and what would soon become many new families with a new generation of children. The problem was quickly addressed with the mass production of pre-fabricated homes in the suburbs, where land was plentiful and cheap. The Levittown housing project on Long Island became synonymous with cookie-cutter style suburban homes, but this was a big improvement over the poor crowded housing people had before. Young people used to living with extended families in aged, cramped housing in the city could now find space, privacy, and a comfortable future in the converted farmlands and prairies surrounding the cities.

GDP growth was robust during the post-war High period with nine years above 4%. This growth reflected strong job growth, rising incomes, and wealth creation in America. There were three mild recessions during this period, but overall the High period was a time of strong economic growth and prosperity. It also was a time of massive transformation to a growing middle class and a consumer-driven economy.

Figure 1-5.

GDP Growth in the U.S. - High Period

Source: Kimberly Amadeo and U.S. Dept of Commerce Bureau of Economic Analysis

Not only did people move to the suburbs, but they moved across country, as generations had done before in covered wagons and in trains, searching for a new beginning. California was the destination for many who moved west in a new gold-rush spirit that made the state the most populous in the country by 1963. Baseball fans in New York watched in disbelief as both their beloved Brooklyn Dodgers and New York Giants moved to Los Angeles and San Francisco respectively.

Politics and Foreign Affairs

The political landscape shifted with the return to prosperity. David Halberstam describes in his book, *The Fifties*, that there was a need to get back to Americanism after the war. A return to the "American way of life"[19] marked a shift to a period of "private interest" in Schlesinger's political-cycle theory and a desire by

Republicans to "get even for The New Deal" and undo the changes that progressives had made since FDR took office in 1933. The government had stepped in during the Great Depression to provide jobs and economic safety nets for the unemployed and impoverished Americans. The Republicans believed that the government had gone too far and had become too big. Others felt that the stock market crash was caused by the concentration of wealth among the top 1% and the lack of wage growth for the middle class to drive consumer spending. An absence of effective bank regulation has also been cited as a cause. However, Eisenhower was a moderate and continued to support the New Deal and expanded social security. Roosevelt's progressive legacy was preserved.

Figure 1-6.

Theory of Cycles	1945	1950	1955	1960	1965
Strauss & Howe - Generational Cycles					
High		High			
Awakening					Awakeni
Unraveling					
Crisis					
Schlesinger - Political					
Public Purpose					Public
Private interest		Private			
Klingberg - Foreign Policy					
Extrovert		Extrovert			
Introvert					

The U.S. was in an 'extroverted' foreign policy mood that had started in 1940 and would respond aggressively with direct action as the world's superpower. The national security focus was on the real external and perceived internal threats to our way of life – the dangers of Communism and Socialism. Vice-President Harry

Truman assumed the presidency following FDR's death in April, 1945. He proclaimed the Truman Doctrine in 1947, promising to help any country that was threatened by Communism. While he surprisingly managed to win a second term in 1948, by 1952 he was deeply unpopular. China had fallen to the Communists in 1949 and the war in Korea ended in a stalemate. He decisively fired General Douglas MacArthur, a national hero from WWII, in 1951 for promoting his own risky if not reckless strategy to bomb China and use Chinese Nationalist troops from Taiwan in the Korean war to Republican lawmakers,– but many in the country favored MacArthur. Truman tested the waters for a second full-term in the New Hampshire primary, but was defeated by Este Kefauver, so he withdrew his name from consideration and convinced Adlai Stevenson, the progressive Governor of Illinois, to run in his place.

The Republicans also needed a fresh face, one who had not been tainted by partisan arguments over the popular New Deal. They turned to an outsider and a war hero, General Dwight D. Eisenhower. Eisenhower campaigned on Truman's failures and defeated Stevenson easily in the 1952 Presidential race, winning 39 states and 55% of the popular vote. The Democrats' liberal political policy had run its course for now, after nearly twenty (20) years. Of the nine (9) states that Stevenson won, seven (7) were in the South, which would switch to Republican candidates in 1964 and for many years afterward in reaction to Democratic support for Civil Rights legislation. The Republicans also briefly controlled the Congress in 1947 and 1953.

Figure 1-7.

The focus was on the American Dream of economic affluence and material well-being, rather than on social ideals. Eisenhower literally paved the way for America's westward expansion with the creation of the nation's interstate highway system. This also contributed to economic development with both construction jobs and productivity gains in logistics for businesses. With the focus on "private matters," as Schlesinger described, a suburban home, a secure job, and large families became a testament to the new High period of stability and social order. Surprisingly, the number of married women working outside the home rose from 17% in 1940 to 32% in 1960. Whether this was precipitated by financial need or personal desire for a career outside the home, a growing minority of women did break from the mold during this period. But even in the face of political differences, foreign conflicts or the hunt for "Reds" (Communists) in the country,

Americans trusted their government. Pew Research surveys showed trust in government above 70% during the High period after they began tracking "trust" in 1958.

Figure 1-8 Trust in Government

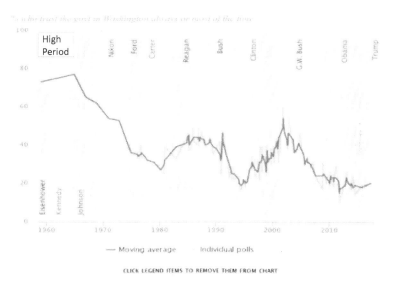

Churches and synagogues followed their congregations to the suburbs. Robert Ellwood noted in his book *The Fifties Spiritual Marketplace: American Religion in a Decade of Conflict,* that during the 1950s nationwide church membership grew at a faster rate than the population, from 57 percent of the U.S. population in 1950 to 63.3 percent in 1960. Churches and synagogues also helped fill a gap in social cohesion that was created when families left their traditional neighborhood communities in the cities for suburbs of nice strangers. Congress supplied additional glue for the religious fabric when it added "under God" to the Pledge of Allegiance in 1954 and made "In God We Trust" the official motto of the country in 1953. While the motto had already been on our currency and coins since 1865, the willingness to punctuate the new civic mood with the prevailing religious norms seemed natural.

These changes to include "God" were made easily in an era of conformity, in spite of the potential conflict they may seem to pose with the separation of church and state called for in the Constitution. America was now the leader of the free world and a (Christian) God had a hand in putting us there. The theme of "under God" as an inexorable part of our pledge of alliance would be raised again, as we approached the next High period in America, when in May, 2017 President Trump delivered a commencement address at Liberty University. He reinforced the "under God" phrase as being the natural order of things and appealed to those who wanted to see more of a blending of church and state values. The issue is not whether "under God" is right or wrong as a policy, but that the themes, policies and social norms that resonate within the nation are more typical in certain generational periods, and they seem to repeat.

Political parties were largely aligned on the primacy of national security on foreign policy issues, so political differences were more pronounced around domestic matters. Divisive approaches to loyalty and anti-communism were fanned domestically after the fall of China to Mao Tse Tung's Communists in 1949 and the absorption of Eastern Europe into the Soviet Union. The Soviets believed that they were entitled to Eastern Europe after the military victory over fascism that they earned through the deaths of millions of their own during WWII. And they also believed that they were conceded this right by Roosevelt and Truman at Yalta and Potsdam. Their autocratic treatment of the people of Eastern Europe after enclosing them behind the Iron Curtain removed any legitimacy for a buffer zone along the border of their homeland that they may have initially garnered.

Sen. Joseph McCarthy of Wisconsin used the power of his Senate Permanent Subcommittee on Investigations to pursue suspected Communists in government and Hollywood in 1954. He crossed a bridge too far when he targeted the U.S. Army and was overly abusive to General Ralph Zwicker in his hearings. His censure and fall from grace followed shortly after. While McCarthy's accusation of the presence of Communists in the U.S. government was never borne out at the time, the successful infiltration of high levels of British Intelligence Services by the "Cambridge Five" (Philby, MacLean, Burgess, Blunt and Cairncross) as Soviet agents in the post-war period suggests that the Soviets (Russians) were quite capable of doing so. The Soviets did, in fact, penetrate U.S. intelligence services in the '80s and '90s, convincing Aldrich Ames (CIA) and Robert Hanssen (FBI) to spy and provide valuable information to them, which resulted in serious national security setbacks for the U.S. Perhaps the Russians just did not get caught earlier during McCarthy's investigative circus.

Foreign policy was focused on two main areas during the High period; containment of Communism and the related nuclear arms race with the Soviet Union. George Kennan, a diplomat with the State Department in Moscow, had written an extensive position paper in 1946 on the need for "containing" the Soviet Union. This policy paper was later published in *Foreign Affairs* magazine in 1947 under the pseudonym "X." In his later memoirs, Kennan wrote that containment, "was not something that I thought we could necessarily do everywhere successfully"[20] and added that "containment of Soviet power was not the containment by military means of a military threat, but the political containment of a political threat."[21] But political containment was a priority as the Communist form of government was in direct contradiction to our democratic and capitalist values.

The High period coincided with an "extroverted" foreign policy period within Klingberg's cycle theory. The U.S. assumed a global leadership role as a military and economic superpower. The Marshall Plan was initiated to rebuild Europe and create a democracy in West Germany to replace fascism. East Germany and Eastern Europe were already secured behind the Iron Curtain. But Berlin was still partitioned into sectors that the Soviets and the West controlled. In the first crisis of the post-war period, the U.S. confronted the Soviet Union aggressively with the Berlin airlift in 1948, when the Soviets blockaded supply routes into Berlin from the West, with the aim to take complete control of Berlin.

Figure 1-9.

Theory of Cycles	1945	1950	1955	1960	1965
Strauss & Howe - Generational Cycles					
High		High			
Awakening					Awakeni
Unraveling					
Crisis					
Schlesinger - Political					
Public Purpose					Public
Private interest		Private			
Klingberg - Foreign Policy					
Extrovert		Extrovert			
Introvert					

The major foreign 'hot spot' during the High period was in North Korea. The Russians had declared war on Japan in August, 1945, and quickly invaded Inner Mongolia and northern Korea. In return for entering the war against Japan in Asia, the Allies agreed to partition Korea along the 38th parallel, tacitly recognizing the respective areas controlled by Soviet and American forces. The seeds were planted for the war that would occur just five years later. The Soviets again tested the U.S. when Stalin green-lighted the invasion of the South by the North. North Korean tanks and infantry swarmed across the 38th parallel in June, 1950 and quickly captured Seoul, but not before President Rhee of South Korea executed over 100,000 civilians suspected of being pro-Communist. The U.S. responded aggressively. Truman sent in U.S. troops and deployment levels quickly rose to nearly 600,000, far lower than in the upcoming war in Vietnam or the nearly 8 million deployed abroad in WWII (chart below).

Figure 1-10.

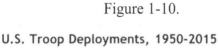

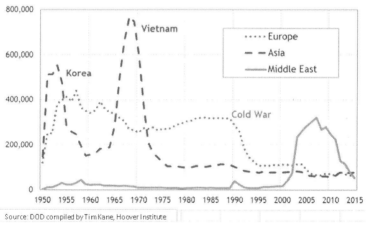

The U.S. pushed the Communists out of the south and continued all the way to Pyongyang when China suddenly sent hundreds of thousands of their soldiers across the border and pushed the Americans back across the 38th parallel. When an armistice was signed in 1953, the border between North and South Korea was exactly where it was before the war started. The war in Korea would have a direct impact on the U.S. policy to contain Communism in Vietnam to prevent the "fall of dominos" ten years later.

The other military conflicts during this High period were waged in Cold War style through proxies in places like Greece and Lebanon. The "extroverted" foreign policy continued with a rapid buildup of nuclear weapons meant to deter the Soviet Union. The nuclear threat posed by the build-up of vastly more powerful atomic bombs along with the means to deliver them across oceans and continents would continue to be the major focus and concern of U.S. foreign policy.

When John F. Kennedy said at his inauguration in 1961 that "the torch has been passed to a new generation of Americans - born in this century, tempered by war, disciplined by a hard and bitter peace,"[22] he was formally announcing the coming-of-age of the Baby Boomers. Former President Eisenhower was then a seventy-year-old war hero and a member of the Lost Generation, born before the turn of the century. The educated, passionate, and handsome John F. Kennedy was also a WWII veteran, but just 44 years old. He was also the first Catholic President, a big shift from the Protestant Presidents who had held the office since the country's founding. Kennedy defeated Nixon by only 120,000 popular votes but carried the Electoral College 303 to 219, even with 15 electoral votes from the south going to Democrat Harry Byrd.

Figure 1-11.

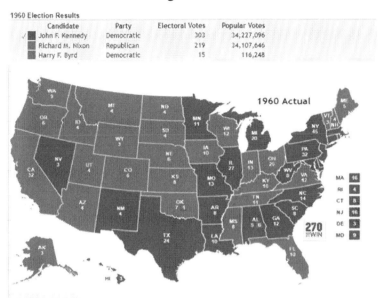

Source: 270towin.com

Kennedy set the tone for his vision in his inauguration speech when he said, "We stand today on the edge of a New Frontier — the frontier of the 1960s, the frontier of unknown opportunities and perils, the frontier of unfilled hopes and unfilled threats . . . Beyond that frontier are uncharted areas of science and space, unsolved problems of peace and war, unconquered problems of ignorance and prejudice, unanswered questions of poverty and surplus."[23] He would form a government with what would be termed by David Halberstam as *"The Best and the Brightest"* which was the title of his best-selling book covering the tumultuous years of the Kennedy and Johnson administrations. Secretary of Defense Robert McNamara, Secretary of State Dean Rusk, and National Security Advisor McGeorge Bundy would all have a decisive impact on escalating the war in Vietnam.

In his brief time as President, Kennedy would not be able to pass major pieces of his domestic policy agenda, but enough cooperation existed between the parties that allowed for some things to get done -- an increase in unemployment benefits, aid to cities for transportation and housing funding for national highways, along with some anti-poverty legislation, yet nothing really major. But with the Cold War in full swing after the bitter war and resulting stalemate at the 38th parallel in Korea, Kennedy would face a serious foreign-policy challenge with the Soviet Union that would come to define his presidency. In April, 1961, the administration green-lighted a C.I.A. plan to overthrow the Communist regime in Cuba using Cuban exiles, which had been developed and funded during the Eisenhower administration. The mission failed due to poor planning and execution. Some in the C.I.A., and many others, blamed Kennedy. The Cubans and Russians responded to this, as well as the presence of American nuclear missiles in Turkey and Italy, by placing nuclear missiles and launch capabilities in Cuba. Kennedy decided against direct military action against Cuba in favor of a naval blockade along with the threat to board any ship attempting to cross it. This brought the two super-powers to the brink of war during thirteen days in October, 1962. A convoy of Russian cargo ships turned around as it approached the blockade. Ultimately, Khrushchev backed down and removed the missiles from Cuba and the U.S. quietly removed their missiles from Turkey. But the world got a very real glimpse of what could result from direct conflict between the U.S. and Soviet Union. The war in Vietnam was just over the horizon, one that Kennedy would not live to see.

Millennial folk band The Lumineers expressed both the hope and disappointment that young Baby Boomers felt with Kennedy's presidency in Charlie Boy, written years later in 2012.

Chapter 2

Awakening Period (1963 – 1980)

"The Second Turning is an Awakening, a passionate era of social and spiritual upheaval, when the civic order comes under attack from a new values regime." [24]

Figure 2-1.

Turning	Period	Families	Child Rearing	Gap in Gender Roles	Trust in Government	Voter Turnout	Social Priorities	New Gen Focus	Wars
				Social Behaviors and Attitudes					
Second Turning	Awakening	Weakening	Under protective	narrowing	declining	declining	rising individualism	fix inner world	controversial

Many key measures of social order plunged during the Awakening period even as rising individualism helped propel progressive ideals. The family unit was torn apart by divorce, Gen X children were under-protected, the gap in gender roles between men and women narrowed significantly, trust in government and voter turnout plunged. The only war would be controversial.

The American mood had shifted on that fateful day in November, 1963. The American High we had experienced since V-J Day in 1945 came to an emotional and abrupt end. The romantic image of Camelot had come to life for a brief period in America and epitomized the positive feelings that Americans had since the G.I.'s came home and the focus returned to family, jobs, and community. The assassination of President Kennedy marked the end of the American High, which had changed the economic life of America for the better in the private sector, but that had neglected investing in the public sector. The result being that many people in the country continued to experience economic and social inequities, as John Kenneth Galbraith described in *The Affluent Society* in 1958.

The status quo faced upheaval across a broad spectrum of issues: women's rights, civil rights, gay rights, environmental concerns, foreign policy, and economic equality. Hippies, communes, drugs, rock n' roll and a new devotion to Mother Earth formed a new social ethos for the generation. Rachel Carson's book, *The Silent Spring* (1962) would propel an environmental movement that stopped DDT from being sprayed on food crops. Young people returned to farms to start what would become an organic food revolution. The gap between genders narrowed as young men grew long hair and everyone donned both flamboyant and/or drab attire. Women demanded to be treated equally.

The Awakening was a direct attack on the mood of the American High and what was perceived as its stagnant, conformist values and norms that had been inculcated in response to the sixteen years of intense crisis people had endured. The economy had boomed and the quality of life had improved for millions of Americans. Many did not understand why anyone would want to change that! Change it did, but not without a forceful counter punch from the Greatest Generation who had won the war and some of those from the next Silent Generation that also liked it just the way it was. But just as conventional social attitudes typified the mood of a High period, so too would a counter-culture mood exemplify the Awakening period. As such, the Awakening period, and the new generation that propelled it forward with their young energy, served as a catalyst to address the unresolved issues simmering below the calm surface of the High period. It was a necessary and predictable response to the period that preceded it.

A new generation had been called to action in Kennedy's inaugural address. The lead cohort of the

Baby Boomers would be turning eighteen when he was assassinated. His words were etched in history, "Ask not what your country can do for you, but what you can do for your country."[25] Yet these words were more a call to service consistent with a High period than the protests, upheaval, and cry for individuality that the generation responded with. Organized protests by a myriad of groups expanded rapidly throughout the period. Many had been neglected or supressed during the High period. Activists of all persuasions called for action on the long-simmering and unresolved issues of women's rights, civil rights, environment concerns, and poverty. The following decades would also see a sharp rise in divorce, abortions, riots, and the assassination of another progressive politician and a civil-rights activist. Student protest took on a force not seen before as campuses swelled with Baby Boomers entering college in greater numbers.

Figure 2-2.

	Awakening Period 1964 - 1980			
	Children	Young Adults	Mid-Life Adults	Elders
Generation	Gen X	Baby Boomers	Silent	G.I.
Archetype	Nomad	Prophet	Artist	Hero

The Prophet archetype, nurtured as indulged children, brings forth an ideal vision of society which they attempt to forge with passion as they come of age. This vision is steeped in spiritual or religious values that prioritize the rights of the individual over the established norms of the society.

The exploding availability of new technology for mass communications in music, television, and film would serve as a new, effective tool for a vocal generation. These mediums provided the activists of the generation the means

to effect change more readily, as musicians such as Bob
Dylan exemplified.

*Dylan trumpeted the radical changes that a new
generation was bringing in 1964 in his prescient
folk song The Times They Are-Changin.*

Trust in government plunged during the Awakening
across four presidencies, driven by the war in Vietnam,
Watergate, the Pentagon Papers, a surge in crime, inflation,
an oil crisis, unemployment, and the prolonged hostage
crisis in Iran.

Figure 2-3 Trust in Government

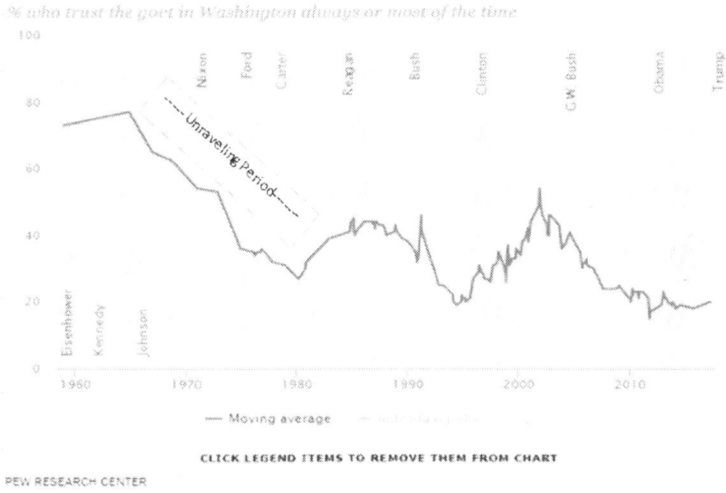

% who trust the govt in Washington always or most of the time

CLICK LEGEND ITEMS TO REMOVE THEM FROM CHART

PEW RESEARCH CENTER

Women and Family

As the Awakening period crossed into the 1970s, our
society was already feeling the reverberations from the
upheaval and domestic conflict. Women and associated

family issues were at the center of what Francis Fukuyama termed *The Great Disruption* in his 1999 book. He described how negative trends in many social indicators occurred throughout Western Europe and the United States during this period. The traditional roles of women and the state of the family had been tightly interwoven in the '50s. Betty Friedan challenged those traditional roles in 1963 with her bestselling book, *The Feminine Mystique*. Friedan went on to form the National Organization for Women (NOW) in 1966 and, along with other groups, helped bring women's issues regarding job discrimination, reproductive rights, and crimes against women to the national spotlight during the Awakening period.

One of the most significant events in history affecting the lives of women was the development of the birth-control pill. The FDA approved use of the pill in 1960 for menstrual disorder, but not contraception. Use of contraception for birth control was illegal in many states, even for married people. Hard to imagine that today. The Supreme Court overturned Connecticut's law banning contraception for married couples on the basis of privacy in Griswold v. Connecticut in 1965. By 1965 over 6 million women were using the pill. Women had control of their reproductive rights in a way never seen before and millions of women began exercising that right. The decision was later applied to unmarried couples in a 1972 case. The wider use of birth control accelerated the decline in the birth rate that had already peaked in 1957. Gen X was being born during the Awakening period, marked by lower births and smaller families. Their youth would be further marked by rising divorce and working single parents. Gen X would respond by refining their skills at self-reliance and earn a reputation as "survivors." The reality television show "Survivor" debuted in 2000; it personified their early life experiences and their coming of age persona of Gen X.

Figure 2-4.

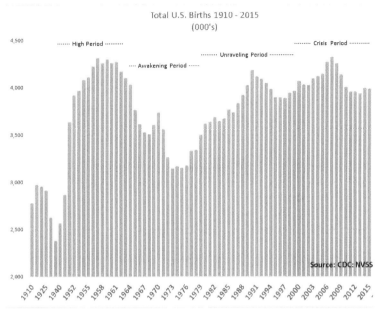

Total U.S. Births 1910 - 2015
(000's)

Women's rights to make pregnancy choices took a giant leap forward with the Supreme Court landmark decision in Roe v. Wade in January, 1973, which legalized the right to have an abortion for women nationwide. Abortions accelerated quickly as did the emotional divisions on both sides of the issue. Any woman who has ever been pregnant must know what a difficult personal decision that is.

Figure 2-5.

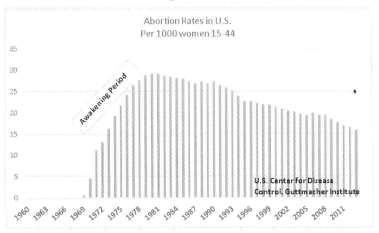

The divorce rate soared during the Awakening as women took flight from unhappy marriages, along with their sexual freedom in the form of a small birth-control pill case that could fit in their purses. States legislatures facilitated the trend by enacting laws which made it easier to attain a divorce. Congress passed the Equal Rights Amendment in 1972, but it was never ratified by the states in spite of repeated extensions of the seven-year time limit set by the Constitution.

Figure 2-6.

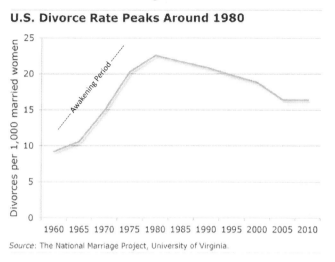

U.S. Divorce Rate Peaks Around 1980

Source: The National Marriage Project, University of Virginia.

Women also began entering the workforce and attending college in greater numbers. In 1963, about 1.8 million women were enrolled in postsecondary education. They comprised about 38 percent of total enrollment. By 1978, women became half of students enrolled in postsecondary education. That trend would continue to rise, reaching almost 12 million women and 57 percent of total by 2012. (Department of Education, 2012, Table 221). While breaking the norms to establish their own identity, women faced sexual and salary discriminations in the workplace that have continued to this day. Films such as *9 to 5* (1980) with Dolly Parton, Lily Tomlin, and Jane Fonda brought a humorous light to a serious problem, the offending boss well portrayed by Dabney Coleman. But the problem was very real and systemic.

Civil Rights

Civil rights issues had started to arise soon after WWII as many blacks had served admirably in the military, but

33

came home to the same racial discrimination that had existed before they left. Rosa Parks had made a brave personal statement in 1955 by refusing to move to the back of the bus. But it was during the Awakening period that civil rights exploded across the country as a national issue. Martin Luther King, Jr. provided the African-American community a much needed spiritual leader who, like Gandhi, preached peaceful protest rather than violence as a means to achieve the dignity and equal rights that the Constitution envisioned and the Civil War was fought to ensure.

In the march on Washington, D.C. in 1963, King delivered his "I have a dream" speech from the Lincoln Memorial to over 200,000 people. In 1964, the murder of three Freedom Riders in Mississippi, two of the whites from the north, attracted greater media attention to civil rights. King led peaceful marches from Birmingham to Selma in 1965. In the first of three marches, police beat Amelia Boynton unconscious and a picture of her lying wounded on the bridge was publicized nationally. Like the Vietnam War, television brought the perverse reality that long pervaded the American culture into people's living rooms. The sight of dogs and fire hoses being turned on men, women, and children who were peacefully marching in Birmingham in 1963 created a national uproar. With President Johnson using his considerable influence, Congress passed the Civil Rights Act in 1964 and the Voting Rights Act in 1965. But subsequent events would show the deep nature of the problem. Poverty, discrimination and poor living conditions would not be easily solved with legislation.

Riots erupted in Watts in 1965 and occurred throughout the country over the next few years. While the hippies celebrated the "Summer of Love" in San Francisco and Monterey in 1967, the blacks would experience "The Long Hot Summer of 1967" with riots in dozens of cities with the most serious occurring in Detroit, Newark, Cincinnati, and Buffalo. While the Congress was deliberating the Civil Rights Act of 1968 to establish fair housing laws for blacks, Martin Luther King, Jr. was assassinated in Memphis. Riots, looting, and arson ignited in many cities. The poor urban areas that had been abandoned by the whites fleeing to the suburbs would be set ablaze following his murder.

Bruce Springsteen captured the hot emotions that existed between the races in 1965, when he was still in high school, in his 1985 song My Hometown.

Progress was made when the first African-American, Thurgood Marshall, was nominated to the Supreme in 1967 by President Johnson. But inequity was still rife throughout the country. At the 1968 Summer Olympic Games in Mexico City, two black American track medal winners stood shoe-less and in black socks on the medals podium and raised their black-gloved fist in the air with heads bowed as the American national anthem played in protest to racial inequality in America. The Awakening period served a vital purpose in elevating the cause of civil rights in the national consciousness and in political action. The social upheaval was a necessary step in achieving greater progress on the issue of civil rights for all. It would evolve further to include rights for the handicapped and people with different sexual-orientations.

Pop Culture

Television shows started the era with the same comfort and stability as seen in the High period. *Lassie, Father Knows Best* and *Andy Griffith* celebrated the important values of family and home, in a way that reinforced traditional roles and norms. As the decade rolled forward, the unresolved issues of the 1950s would be played out in a variety of sit-coms. The character Archie Bunker in *All in the Family* personified every negative stereotype possible. Sit-coms traced the evolution of women's role in American culture as Mary Tyler Moore went from being Rob Petrie's dutiful wife in *The Dick Van Dyke Show* to a single working woman in *The Mary Tyler Moore Show* in 1970. African-American Diahann Carroll had recently pioneered this role for all women as a widowed, single mom in *Julia* in 1968. Other television shows emerged with black families as the focal point in *Sanford and Son, The Jeffersons,* and *Good Times.* Television was reflecting back to Americans the social change that was rolling across the country.

Films would also reflect the changing times, with non-conformists as the hero and main protagonist; *Cool Hand Luke, Butch Cassidy and the Sundance Kid, The Outlaw Josey Wales, Dirty Harry,* and *The Godfather* personified examples of the "anti-heroes" of the Awakening period. Paul Newman's character in *Cool Hand Luke* voiced the sentiment of the generation when he said, "What we have here, is a failure to communicate."[26] Ken Kesey's novel *One Flew Over the Cuckoo's Nest* became a highly acclaimed film in 1975 portraying Jack Nicholson as a common criminal trying to keep his sanity in a mental institution.

The coming-of-age-movie that defined the new (Baby Boomer) generation was *The Graduate.* In that seminal film of its time, Benjamin Braddock was a disillusioned college graduate who rejected the neighborly advice to pursue a career in "plastics," the dual-meaning of which may have reflected Awakening perceptions of the dull, plastic culture of the recent High period. (In 2004, the word "plastic" would take on yet another meaning in the Millennial-era movie *Mean Girls*.) The unbounded views on sexuality during the Awakening were also on display and were blithely characterized as Benjamin explained simply to Mr.

Robinson regarding his affair with Mrs. Robinson in *The Graduate*, "It didn't mean anything. We might just as well have been shaking hands."[27] Mr. Robinson's retort was one of my favorites, "You'll pardon me if I don't shake hands with you."[28]

The Cold War and 1950's male-female stereotypes were vividly portrayed in the popular James Bond films of the period. Sexual scenes with nudity and violence became more prominent in films as the period progressed, leading to the Motion Picture Association of America to install a rating system in 1968 to warn parents about the films their children might see. As the Awakening period upended the lives of people across the country, George Lucas brilliantly tapped into a deep nostalgia and yearning that mainstream audiences had for the "simple life" that personified the prior High period. *American Graffiti* was released in 1973, and portrayed life in small-town America in 1962. The coming-of-age film captured young Baby Boomers graduating high school just before turning to the Awakening period, the Kennedy assassination, and the start of the Vietnam War and the counter-culture. The nostalgic themes along with the music, cars, and school dances captivated audiences shaken by the events of the previous ten years.

At the other end of the social, political, and emotional spectrum was the movie *MASH*, released in 1970. While *MASH* humorously depicted the experiences of a mobile army surgical hospital (MASH) in Korea, its satirical social commentary was aimed at the Vietnam War and the many in the country that had come to question why we were there. The irreverent behavior and attitudes of Doctors "Hawkeye" Pierce and "Duke" Forrest, who arrive at the MASH unit in a stolen jeep. Along with "Trapper John" McIntyre, they attempt to transform the culture of the MASH to one reminiscent of a college fraternity party while diligently caring for the wounded. The camp, like

America at that time, was split between those who wanted to upend the status quo and those who wanted to vigorously maintain it. This type of film was possible during an Awakening period, but consider how such a satirical comedy about the military (and the war) would be received during our Crisis period today.

John Wayne wanted to portray a more patriotic version of the Vietnam War in *The Green Berets* (1968) filmed in 1967 just before the Tet Offensive and the My Lai Massacre swung public opinion further against the war. *The Deerhunter* (1978) took a much darker and more serious look at the effects the Vietnam War had on the lives of a trio of steelworkers and their loved ones from a small working-class town in Pennsylvania. Francis Ford Coppola adapted Joseph Conrad's *Heart of Darkness* from the Congo to Vietnam in *Apocalypse Now* (1979) to depict the story of a U.S. Army Special Forces Colonel who had gone insane and was running a rogue vigilante operation from Cambodia.

Music became a focal point for the generation to distinguish themselves from the Silent generation and gave voice to protests of all kinds. Bob Dylan led the expansion of social protest in the '60s, following in the footsteps of Woody Guthrie, Pete Seeger, and Johnny Cash who had their start in the decades before. Joan Baez sang songs of protest and social justice and gave voice to women in the process. Other women like Judy Collins, Joni Mitchell, and Janis Joplin had a major impact on the period with their voices, lyrics, and activism.

While blacks were seeking social justice through the civil rights movement, black musicians were achieving prominence and gaining mainstream acceptance with the epic success of the Motown record label in the 60's. Founded by Barry Gordy, premier artists such as The Supremes, The Four Tops, The Temptations, Stevie Wonder, Marvin Gaye and the Jackson 5 produced an endless stream of #1 hits as black pop and R&B music exploded. Motown helped bridge the racial divide between blacks and whites with music which blanketed the radio airwaves and record stores across America. Black music found a place in white America's households even as their neighhoods were still far apart.

Rock n' roll quickly rose to prominence in the 60s as the "British Invasion"' began, led by The Beatles and The Rolling Stones and countless others. The Awakening Period was occurring in Britain and Western Europe as well. The evolution of the Awakening period could be traced in the longer hair, mod clothes, the rising use of drugs and the themes of their music. The release of *Sgt. Pepper's Lonely Hearts Club Band* in 1967 marked a seismic shift in complexity of the Beatles' music and in the social culture in America.

The Summer of Love had arrived in Northern California and the counter-culture was reaching a peak. Peter Max blended colors with the Summer of Love to produce his artwork. Andy Warhol had used the simple but ubiquitous Campbell Soup in his debut of pop artwork in 1962. Consumer-product companies had to speak to their new consumers to reflect the prevailing culture. Even the soft drink company 7-Up was able to revolutionize their clear soda in 1969, positioning it as the "Uncola" in a brilliant marketing campaign, consistent with the prevailing ethos of the counter-culture.

Crime

The crime rate is another key indicator of the level of social order in society. Total crime rates, including both property and violent crime, rose sharply through the Awakening period, soaring from 2,100 per 100,000 population to a peak of 5,950 per 100,000 population in 1980 (chart). Prison population increased from about 200,000 in 1963 to over 300,000 by 1980. It seemed that the country had fallen into a criminal abyss and insanity was rampant. A Presidential Crime Commission was ordered by Johnson in response. Nixon campaigned and won on an anti-crime platform.

Figure 2-7.

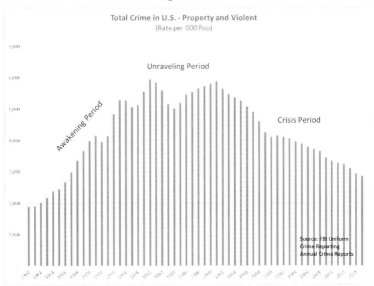

The most famous and heinous crime of the era may well have been the murder of actress Sharon Tate and others by Charlie Manson and his followers in 1969. It cast a pall around the free-loving youth of the era as Manson and his cult resembled everyday hippies. Charles Whitman, a former Marine, climbed to the top of the bell tower on the University of Texas campus with a rifle in 1966 and killed thirteen people below who he caught in his cross-hairs. Richard Speck sent chills through the country when he skulked through a dormitory in Chicago and killed eight student nurses. Albert DeSalvo, "The

Boston Strangler," raped and strangled eleven women. The public was understandably shaken by these brutal and highly publicized murders. The sense of safety expected in our homes, schools, and streets was eroded. Trust in government fell with the rise in crime.

Many theories have been advanced, but no clear, definitive explanation has been provided for the crime boom that spanned nearly three decades. The demographic increase in the number of young males, the counter-culture itself, rock n' roll, drugs, inner city poverty – all have been offered as causal factors. The Presidential Crime Commission noted "what appears to be happening…is that parental, and especially paternal, authority over young people is becoming weaker."[29] Steven Pinker, Harvard College Department of Psychology, wrote in *Decivilization in the 1960's*, that "spontaneity, self-expression, and a defiance of inhibitions became cardinal virtues."[30] As the crime rate has increased during previous Awakening and Unraveling periods, it is fair to say that the social upheaval that accompanies those periods is affected by the persona of the generations who come of age during them.

Politics and Foreign Policy

In a continuation of the foreign policy of containment developed by George Kennan in the 1940s, political and military leaders in the 1960s were vigilant about the expansion of communism around the world and pursued a policy of containing it. The threats that Truman saw in Greece and Korea, Eisenhower saw in Lebanon, and Johnson would see in the Dominican Republic and Vietnam. Often at the expense of supporting repressive military or authoritarian regimes, they served as the Cold War alternatives to direct confrontation with the Soviet Union and the massive casualties experienced in WWII, all the more serious with the advent of the nuclear weapons. The U.S. was still in Schlesinger's "extroverted" foreign policy mood when we expanded the war in Vietnam. But that foreign policy mood would face opposition from an Awakening mood at home, driven by the new Baby Boomer generation coming-of-age. In comparison, the Silent generation responded in a predictable and dutiful way to the Korean War during the High period. The "extroverted mood" was soon to shift to a prolonged "introverted" mood, chastened by the painful military lesson in Vietnam.

Figure 2-8.

Theory of Cycles	1945	1950	1955	1960	1965	1970	1975	1980
Strauss & Howe - Generational Cycles								
High	High							
Awakening					Awakening			
Unraveling								
Crisis								
Schlesinger - Political Focus								
Public Purpose					Public			
Private interest		Private						Privat
Klingberg - Foreign Policy Moods								
Extrovert	Extrovert							
Introvert						Introvert		

The war in Vietnam would be seen in color on nightly television and served during dinner time by the respected and trusted news anchors of the three major networks. What had started out as a short-term effort to reinforce a "fledgling democracy" against communism in Asia, evolved into an unpopular, costly and prolonged war. Unlike the warm welcome that soldiers received when returning from wars during the previous (and future) crisis periods, these veterans were sadly greeted with rancor that was really meant for the government and policies that sent them there.

Springsteen again captured the sentiment felt by a troubled teen sent off to Vietnam in his ballad about life in America, My Hometown.

President Johnson expanded the conflict in Vietnam while also trying to launch his Great Society, a domestic-policy agenda consistent with Democratic ideals and the New Deal protections that FDR championed. The cost and political turmoil of the war eroded his ability to do either well. Protests against the war escalated right along with the number of young men drafted to serve in Vietnam. Deferments were available for those who could afford college.

Figure 2-9.

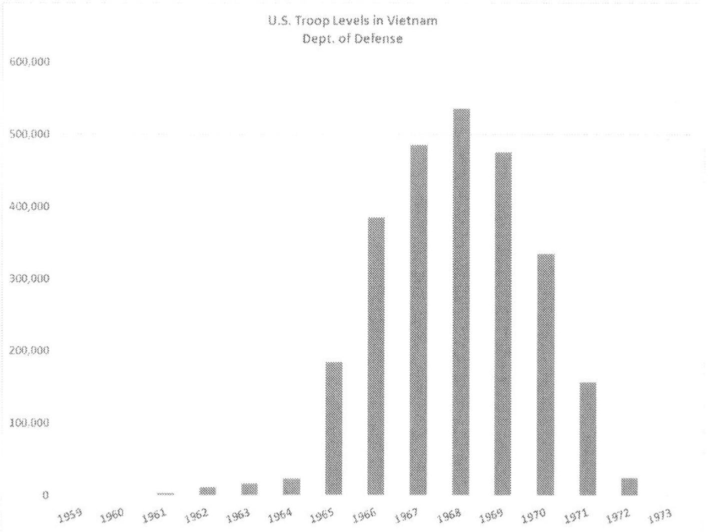

U.S. Troop Levels in Vietnam
Dept. of Defense

The war was seen by many as a continuation of the failed colonialism of the French there previously, rather than as a necessary step to prevent the fall of dominos in Southeast Asia. There did not appear to be a direct threat to U.S. national security from a civil war in a small Asian country. The anti-war movement included not just students, but millions of people from all corners of America. Protests took the form of a "teach-in" at the University of Michigan in 1965 to large marches in San Francisco and New York in 1967. The unpopular war and on-going protests eventually wore on President Johnson. After his loss in the New Hampshire primary to anti-war advocate Eugene McCarthy, Johnson went on national television to announce that "he would not seek, and would not accept" the Democratic nomination for President in 1968. Like President Truman, he rose to the presidency after the death of a sitting President and would only serve one full term of his own, both deciding not to seek a second term after a loss in their party's first primary in New Hampshire.

This opened the door for Vice-President Hubert Humphrey and others to pursue the presidency. Robert Kennedy had the support of young people, Catholics and minorities along with immense emotional sentiment for his murdered brother. At a time when only 14 states held primaries and the leaders of the Democratic Party held sway over who would be nominated, Kennedy won a major victory in the California primary in June, with important Illinois scheduled soon after. But following his victory speech, Bobby was assassinated in the kitchen of the Ambassador hotel in Los Angeles. Protests and police violence would mar the Democratic National Convention in Chicago in August where Hubert Humphrey was awarded the nomination.

The "silent majority" reasserted themselves during the Awakening period in electing the more conservative Nixon. Although Humphrey lost by less than a million votes (out of 70 million cast), Nixon won a huge electoral victory as George Wallace ran as an Independent and carried the south in response to the civil-rights legislation that Johnson and the Democrats had pursued. But even taking the South would not have been enough electoral votes for Humphrey. Unlikely at best for a northern liberal.

Figure 2-10.

The Vietnam War would continue to be in the forefront of the news and public debate. The My Lai Massacre of hundreds of civilians by U.S. soldiers in March, 1968 was kept from the public until it was finally revealed in November, 1969. Although Nixon began troop withdrawals, he escalated the war with bombings in neighboring Cambodia in 1970 to eliminate enemy sanctuaries. Millions of people back home protested in response. The Ohio National Guard was called out in response to a large protest at Kent State University in 1970. Several Guardsmen fired into the crowd killing four, sparking greater tensions at campuses across the country. Soon after, Crosby, Stills, Nash, and Young memorialized those who died in their anti-war song *Ohio*. *The New York Times* published the Pentagon Papers in 1971, which detailed massive and systematic lies and deceptions by the Johnson administration about the events and conduct of the war. The war appeared to be unwinnable, young men were coming home in body bags, and the government had lied to the American people.

Troop levels fell significantly during Nixon's first term. He campaigned for his second term on a gradual withdrawal from Vietnam. He defeated liberal Democrat George McGovern in a massive landslide in 1972, securing almost 20 million votes more than his opponent and winning every state except Massachusetts and the District of Colombia. But voter turnout plunged to 55%. Voter turnout is another meaningful measure of social order. Nixon had been negotiating with the North Vietnamese prior to the election and concluded the Paris Peace Accords in January, 1973. The war in Vietnam was over but Nixon's presidency, and his legacy, would soon be overshadowed by the Watergate break-in, his role in the cover-up and subsequent resignation in 1974 to avoid impeachment. Gerald Ford assumed the presidency and pardoned Nixon to put the turmoil behind the country. The decision was unpopular with many who wanted to see Nixon prosecuted for his crimes.

Jimmy Carter, a former Governor of Georgia, defeated Ford in a close election in 1976, the last time a Democrat won the state of Texas. He was intelligent, had a gentile manner, and appealed to those who wanted change. The economy had slowed down and Ford lost votes with many for his pardon of Nixon. Voter turnout in the election fell further to 54%. The American electorate was detached and distrustful of government.

Figure 2-11.

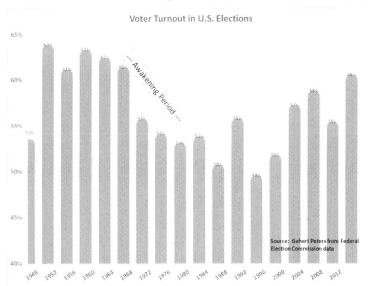

Voter Turnout in U.S. Elections

Carter's well-intentioned Presidency was doomed by the reemergence of rapidly rising inflation and unemployment and the taking of hostages at the U.S. Embassy in Tehran after the overthrow of the U.S.-supported Shah and the imposition of Islamic rule under the Ayatollah Khomeini. The major networks led off every prime-time news cast with a count of the number of days that the hostages had been held. It was a slow Chinese water-torture for President Carter's presidency as the number of days continued to climb past 400.

Economy

The strong economic growth of the 1950s largely carried over into the 1960s. Unemployment remained low. But the 1970s would bring several shocks to the U.S. economy. The first arrived in 1973 when O.P.E.C, the oil-producing cartel, cut production and imposed an embargo on the U.S.

in retaliation for the U.S. support of Israel during the Yom Kippur War with Arab states. Corn, wheat, and soybean prices also skyrocketed due to poor weather and an increase in global demand driven by large purchases from the Soviet Union to compensate for their low crop production. The combined impact of the spikes in oil, grains, and oilseed prices drove inflation to nearly 12%. President Ford's slogan of "Whip Inflation Now' (WIN) did little to reassure the beleaguered public. Unemployment quickly rose to 9% by 1975 and helped Carter defeat Ford in 1976.

Figure 2-12.

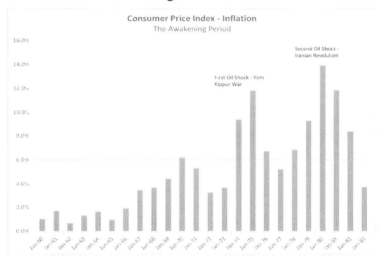

The second oil shock came in 1979 and this one would ultimately doom the Carter Presidency. The U.S. and U.K. had installed Mohammad Reza Pahlavi as the Shah of Iran in 1941 after his father's Prime Minister, Mohammad Mosaddegh, had nationalized the oil industry there. The Shah was later overthrown in the Islamic Revolution in 1979, which resulted in a reduction in oil production. The Iran-Iraq war followed in 1980 and much larger production cuts occurred in both countries. Global oil prices doubled and inflation soared again.

The national mood and trust in government continued to fall to new lows with the rise in inflation and unemployment and with the passing of each humiliating day that the hostages from the U.S. Embassy were held. The disaster at Three-Mile Island in March 1979 compounded people's fear that nuclear power was unsafe and bred a growing opposition to building more plants. The prevailing sense was that our government and institutions were failing us.

Figure 2-13 Trust in Government

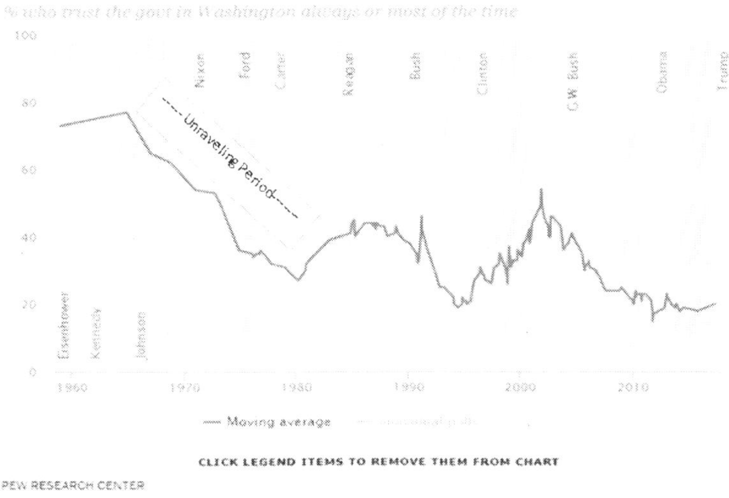

PEW RESEARCH CENTER

The Awakening period had raged on for nearly seventeen years and had served a vital purpose in arousing the social, spiritual, and political consciousness of America. Civil rights, women's rights, and environmental causes were championed by a new generation. Students and many of their elders protested the Vietnam War and the media helped reveal a false narrative advanced by the government.

Democracy was vibrant and alive in America with the vocal participation of its citizens and a free press. But the energy was draining from the period like oil from a leaking engine. The public was tired of upheaval. Change was in the air and the mood would soon be shifting.

Chapter 3

Unraveling Period (1981 – 2001)

"The Third Turning is an Unraveling, a downbeat era of strengthening individualism and weakening institutions, when the old civic order decays and the new values regime implants."[31]

Figure 3-1.

				Social Behaviors and Attitudes					
Turning	Period	Families	Child Rearing	Gap in Gender Roles	Trust in Government	Voter Turnout	Social Priorities	New Gen Focus	Wars
Third Turning	Unraveling	Weak	Tightening	Minimum	Low	Low	max individualism	do what feels right	inconclusive

An unraveling period is a time of maximum individualism; family structure is weak but child rearing is beginning to tighten; the gap in gender roles is at a minimum; trust and voter turnout is at a low point, as is the sense of community. Starbucks recognized the decline in a sense of community in the '90s and positioned their coffeehouses as the "third place" after home and work. They created a sense of community that resonated with the public in a time of broad alienation. Wars would be inconclusive and spill into the next period.

The Unraveling period would mark the coming of age of Gen X. The lead cohort was turning 18 when Reagan took office in 1981. But the media would not pay much attention to them for a while. The Baby Boomers were still the center of attention. Gen X would be greeted with a staggering recession in 1982 when unemployment rose to 10.8%, just when they were first getting out of college and looking for jobs. Gen X would finally be discovered in 1990 but the attention was not flattering.

The new generation had a rough-and-tumble reputation with the media and the general public. A grim perspective of relationships was portrayed in the movie *Reality Bites (1994),* punctuated by the prevalence of the grunge scene, hip-hop music and AIDs. Their music echoed their sense of estrangement from society.

The Clash expressed a generation's rage in 1979 at the unraveling social order they inherited, and personified, in their youth in London's Calling.

Figure 3-2.

	Unraveling Period 1981 - 2001			
	Children	Young Adults	Mid-Life Adults	Elders
Generation	Gen Y	Gen X	Baby Boomers	Silent
Archetype	Hero	Nomad	Prophet	Artist

The Nomads, unprotected as children, grew up indifferent to the bad reputation attributed to them and focused their attention on survival as pragmatic warriors who are unbound from their time and place. They face problems head on.

Figure 3-3.

Source: Time magazine, 1990

An Unraveling period "often opens on a note of good cheer and renewed confidence, but the mood invariably sours."[32] The young U.S. Olympic hockey team had upset the heavily favored Soviet team in February 1980 at Lake Placid to advance to the finals. The country was united behind their young hockey team. Chants of *"USA, USA"* reverberated throughout the country. The mood was upbeat. President Reagan had been working behind the scenes with the Iranians after his election in November 1980, and on inauguration day, the 52 hostages were freed after 444 days in captivity. Six months later, Charles and Diana were married in a storybook wedding between a prince and a princess. In the spring of 1981, a Gallup poll indicated that 48% of the public believed they would be financially better off in the next 12 months.

The mood did indeed sour rather quickly after that. The U.S. dropped into a deep recession for seventeen months from July 1981 to November 1982 as the Federal

Reserve under Paul Volker, significantly raised interest rates to breakthe inflation cycle. Unemployment rose from 7% to nearly 11%. In spite of the poor economy, trust in government rose during the Reagan Presidency, but was still in the low 40's, lower than during the Nixon administration.

Figure 3-4 Trust in Government

% who trust the gov't in Washington always or most of the time

PEW RESEARCH CENTER

The mood in the country had shifted decisively from the desire for social change during the Awakening period in the '60s and '70s. The Awakening period had been successful in challenging the social norms of the 1950s with progress in women's rights, civil rights, and environmental action; but the breakdown in the family and plunging trust in institutions would extract a growing price on the society at large and on Gen X in particular. Divorce rates had peaked in 1980 and Gen X children were frequently left to fend for themselves. Characterized by Strauss & Howe as the "Survivor" generation and as "latch-key" kids by others, Gen X came-of-age in the decade that personal computers were commercialized, cementing their generation's enduring relationship with technology. Apple heralded this new era of digital convenience and productivity with a Super Bowl ad in 1984 which promised enhanced personal freedom rather than the stifling monotony of the Big Brother state, in a twist on George Orwell's dystopian novel *1984*. Orwell wrote *1984* during the last High period in 1949, when a mood of conformity and stability prevailed in the U.S. But in comparison, the Soviet Union had imposed its own version of a utopian world, enforced by an authoritarian state security apparatus. Decades later it might seem ironic that the technology companies might seem like Big Brother themselves.

Other events during the Unraveling period served to reinforce a feeling that society and government had limited control over public safety and security. Gen X grew up with a growing tolerance for gay rights and a deadly virus. The AID's virus was identified in 1981, and would go on to kill over 39 million people worldwide by 2014, according to the CDC. The Challenger exploded on take-off in 1986, killing all seven aboard. A nuclear reactor in Chernobyl melted down and released toxic radioactive material into the atmosphere. Terrorism continued to expand as a method of achieving disparate political ends. A bombing of the peacekeepers barracks in Lebanon by Islamic Jihad Organization would kill hundreds of U.S. and French soldiers. A bomb exploded on Pan Am flight #103 in 1988 as it ascended over Lockerbie, Scotland after take-off from London Heathrow airport, killing all 259 people aboard and 11 more on the ground as the debris rained over the town. Agents of the Libyan government, directed by Muammar Gaddafi, were later implicated in the bombing, which was in retaliation for an on-going conflict between the U.S. and Libya. A 1998 bombing of the U.S. Embassy in Tanzania and Kenya would also kill hundreds. An attack on the warship USS Cole would follow in 2000, as Al Qaeda emerged as a primary enemy of the country.

Women and Family

The women's movement of the Awakening period had raised the visibility of a range of women's issues; abortion and birth control, careers and equal-pay, domestic violence, marriage and divorce. It also highlighted the contradictory expectations for women to care for the family as well as themselves and the need for greater sharing of responsibility for child-rearing. These issues etched a deeper impression on America's social fabric as the Unraveling period unfolded. As more women moved into the workplace, complaints of sexual harassment rose with them. Hopes were still high when Geraldine Ferraro became the first woman nominated by a political party for the office of Vice-President at the Democratic convention in 1984 and real changes were expected.

Births rates had plunged during Gen X's childhood in the '60s, but resurged again in the '80s as Baby Boomers started to have children. Gen Y was being born; some called it an "echo boom."

Figure 3-5.

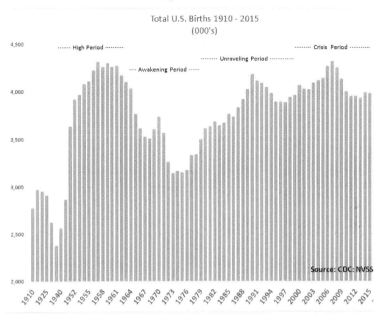

Total U.S. Births 1910 - 2015
(000's)

Abortion rates had risen throughout the Awakening period but finally began to decline in the Unraveling period. Birth control was becoming available and the effective use was more prevalent. This helped to prevent many unplanned pregnancies which had a beneficial effect on reducing abortions.

Figure 3-6.

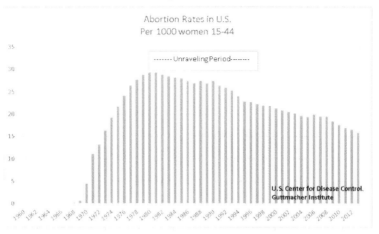

Civil Rights

African-Americans made progress with civil rights legislation in the Awakening Period but racism was by no means subdued. The country would watch the video on national news of Rodney King's beating in March 1991 by Los Angeles police officers and later see them acquitted of any wrongdoing. The Unraveling period would see the rise of crack cocaine in the black community, which contributed to the rise in murder rates of black youth. Pop culture imitated reality and hip hop and gangsta rap became prominent.

The Bill Cosby Show reflected an aspirational middle class life style for blacks that some would come to realize but was beyond the grasp for many in the Midwest areas blighted by job losses from globalization. (Later accusations that Cosby drugged and sexually assaulted many women would ruin his reputation). Incomes of blacks fared better on both coasts, but the gap between whites and blacks was still wide. In 1967, combined earnings for two-income black families was 71% of that for the average white family. By 1990, black families were earning 84.7% of what whites earned. In families where the husband was the only wage earner, the gap was wider.

Figure 3-7.

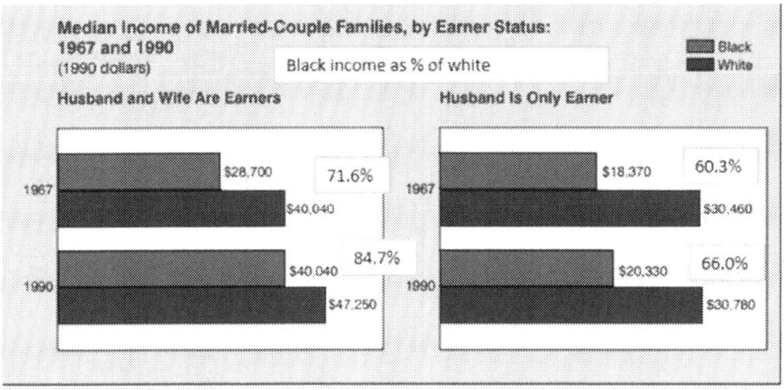

Median Income of Married-Couple Families, by Earner Status: 1967 and 1990 (1990 dollars)

Black income as % of white

■ Black
■ White

Husband and Wife Are Earners			Husband Is Only Earner		
1967	$28,700	71.6%	1967	$18,370	60.3%
	$40,040			$30,460	
1990	$40,040	84.7%	1990	$20,330	66.0%
	$47,250			$30,780	

Source: U.S. Census Bueau, 1993

Blacks would rise to national prominence in positions of power when General Colin Powell was appointed Chairman of the Joint Chiefs of Staff and conservative Clarence Thomas rose to the Supreme Court. Director Spike Lee received an Academy Award nomination for Best Screenplay in 1989 for *Do the Right Thing* and followed with *Malcolm X,* an impactful biographical drama on the leader of the Nation of Islam. The civil-rights movement tried to regain the national spotlight on black issues during the Unraveling period, which culminated in the Million Man March on Washington, D.C. in 1995.

Crime

Although the crime rate had plateaued in the '80s and began a rapid decline in 1991, the state prison population nearly doubled from 750,000 in 1991 to 1.3 million in

2015. The prison population increased as a result of changes in public policy. This included more prison sentences, lengthening time served, "three strikes" laws, and reductions in parole or early release. Perhaps the single greatest force behind the growth of the prison population was the national "War on Drugs." Use of crack and powdered cocaine had become widespread. The number of incarcerated drug offenders had increased twelvefold since 1980. Blacks bore a disproportionate share of the increased incarceration for drug use. Incarceration of more people in spite of the flattening crime rate may have given some people the sense they were secure, while other measures of social order were falling.

Figure 3-8.

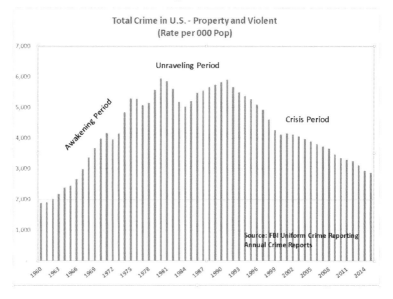

Crime took a cruel twist in the 1990's with the rise of gun violence and domestic terrorism. Timothy McVeigh and Terry Nichols killed 168 when they exploded a truck bomb in front of a Federal building in Oklahoma City. In

1999 two high school student took automatic weapons to Columbine High School and went on a murderous rampage, killing thirteen students and teachers. The senseless killings would continue to escalate in the new millennium, raising an on-going debate over the need for tighter background checks for gun ownership.

Pop Culture

Pop culture experienced dramatic shifts in the Unraveling period as well. The Baby Boomers seemed to always suck up all the oxygen in the room and Gen X was basically ignored, or abandoned, by others. They wanted to be seen and heard in their unique way. As Gen X began to turn 18 in 1980, a glimpse of their collective persona was visible in some of the coming-of-age movies at the time. *Risky Business* (1983) personified the lack of parental oversight that Gen X experienced, as well as the pragmatic business acumen they would become known for. This under-parenting sentiment would later be voiced by the band Oasis in 1996.

> *Gen X was termed latch-key kids as they came home from school unsupervised and smoked pot in Oasis' Champagne Supernova.*

A cross-section of the generation was aptly portrayed by four high-school students in the infamous *Breakfast Club*, along with a classic soundtrack. (1985). John Hughes captured a more convivial and light-hearted attitude with *Ferris Bueller's Day Off* (1986). *Risky Business* gave way to a more serious look at some of the career-minded in *Wall Street* (1987), where the values of greed were laid bare. But it was *Dirty Dancing* (1987) that combined music, dance, and sexuality in a way that Gen X enthusiastically embraced. The 1983 film *War Games* blended the rising threat from nuclear weapons with the new power of computers as a young hacker mistakes reality for a simulation, a film based in part on actual events. Gen X's love of technology would evolve further. The Vietnam War would be presented on film to Gen X in an unvarnished manner which they readily related to. On one hand was, *Good Morning Vietnam (1987)* which, like *MASH*, took a satirical and comedic look at an unpopular war, contrasted with *Platoon* (1986), *Full Metal Jacket* (1987) and *Born on the Fourth of July* (1989), which revealed the reality and brutality of war without romanticizing it.

But perhaps no single event in pop culture more epitomized Gen X than the advent of MTV in 1981, along with its iconic montage of the moon landing. The development of 24-hour news for the older generation by CNN in 1980 paved the way for 24-hour music videos for the younger one. Cyndi Lauper helped pioneer the music video genre and the tone was captured succinctly by Dire Straits in the refrain "I want my MTV" in their 1985 song *Money for Nothing* on their multi-platinum album *Brothers in Arms*. Musical genres spanned rock, pop, punk, rap, and grunge and reflected the generation's desire for raw, honest connection with their music. Their musicians were as unique to their generational persona as The Beatles and The Stones were to the Baby Boomers. Musicians such as Prince, Madonna, Michael Jackson, U2, The Cure, The Police, Nirvana, Pearl Jam, Beck, Dr. Dre, Green Day, Alanis Morissette, and Radiohead represent a small spectrum of Gen X's unique musical era.

The '90s also saw the devolution of objective journalism in the news industry. The combination of 24/7 cable news and the desire to milk more profit from the news division had a discernable impact on the quality of the news itself. Meaningful reporting from the field was subordinated as talking heads at the studio proliferated on television. By 1996, Fox News became the voice of the conservatives while CNN was a vocal platform for the progressive point of view. Rupert Murdoch had hired Roger Ailes, a former media consultant for the Republican Party, as CEO of the head the new Fox News Channel. Worse yet, it seemed that the stories and content were selected and presented in a way that supported a foregone conclusion the networks wanted to convey. Even more, that stories would be told in a voice that supported their viewpoints. A tone of condescending superiority was taken by both sides. Our media had become as biased and polarized as our government.

Politics and Foreign Affairs

The landslide election of conservative Republican Ronald Reagan in 1980 marked the end of the Awakening period and the start of what Strauss & Howe termed the "Unraveling" period. After seventeen years of unending social turmoil, the mood would be to receive a short-term lift before "public trust ebbs amid a fragmenting culture, harsh debates over values and weakening civic habits."[33] Reagan's campaign slogan in 1980 was "Let's Make America Great Again." Reagan defeated Carter by over 8 million votes and handed him a crushing defeat in the Electoral College. The Carter/Mondale ticket managed to win only their respective home states and five others. For the 48 years from 1933 until 1981, the Democrats had controlled both the House and the Senate except for two 2-year periods. The Republicans were firmly in control with a mandate to pursue a more conservative agenda. The reality of a devolving social ordermotivated a concerned voter base to elect a more conservative politicians to help restore stability. But many stayed homefrom the polls in frustration with government.

Figure 3-9.

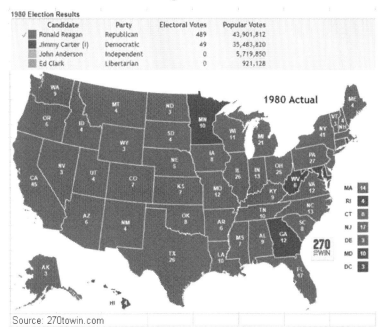

The cartoon (below) from the *San Francisco Examiner* in 1984 humorously depicts the political evolution of a Baby Boomer voter from 1968 to 1980, as they moved from one stage of life to the next. Certainly many people remained dedicated to the Democratic Party and their progressive ideals, but the cartoon effectively captures a cultural shift that did occur, which resulted in Republican control of the White House throughout the '80s and a focus on the economy. Reagan was against abortion, affirmative action, and government regulation.

Figure 3-10.

Source: San Francisco Examiner,

The Reagan presidency and conservative movement was not without its own problems. It was discovered in 1986 that Oliver North, a staff member of the National Security Council in the White House, had engineered an illegal arms sale to Iran to fund the Contras insurgency against the communist Sandinista government in Nicaragua. The Secretary of Defense, Casper Weinberger, National Security Advisor Robert McFarland, National Security Advisor John Poindexter, and Assistant Secretary of State Elliott Abrams were the most senior administration officials charged. After President's Regan's two terms, George H.W. Bush was elected President in 1988; he pardoned several Reagan administration officials while others had their convictions overturned on appeal. Trust in government plunged during Bush's first two years in office to the low levels seen during the Carter administration.

International events mirrored the Unraveling that was occurring in the U.S. but to a much different degree. While the social structure in the U.S. was under pressure, the entire political and economic structure in the Soviet Union collapsed in 1991. Their crisis period began a full ten years before the U.S. would begin its own. The fear of nuclear annihilation during the 1980s dissipated first with the cracks in the Berlin Wall in 1989 and then with the dissolution of the Soviet Union in 1991. Gorbachev had unwittingly unleashed a power which he would soon lose control of. The arms race and a steep decline in the price of oil worked in tandem with Gorbachev's attempts at political reform to precipitate the fall of the Soviet Union.

The implications for the United States were enormous. Reductions in military spending and a booming economy would drive the U.S. toward a budget surplus and we would stand as the world's sole superpower. As George Kennan, the architect of the post-war "containment" policy had written regarding the Soviet Union, "stand up to them and give the hands of time a chance to work."[34] His words were prescient. The foreign policy of the U.S. would soon shift focus from an arms race and containing Communism to securing access to oil in the Middle East and combatting terrorism. In the late '80s, the U.S. was still in the "introverted" foreign policy mood that had started in 1970. There would be no major military actions during the "introvert" period, even as it extended into the Unraveling

Figure 3-11

Theory of Cycles	1965	1970	1975	1980	1985	1990	1995	2000	2005
Strauss & Howe - Generational Cycles									
High									
Awakening	Awakening								
Unraveling					Unraveling				
Crisis									Crisis
Schlesinger - Political Focus									
Public Purpose	Public					Public			
Private interest				Private					
Klingberg - Foreign Policy Moods									
Extrovert								Extrovert	
Introvert		Introvert							

The '80s had also seen China experiment with capitalism under Premier Deng Xiaoping. The market reforms benefitted some but hurt others, but would be China's first step to eventually challenging the U.S. as an economic power. With the new economic freedoms came student protests for greater democracy and freedom of speech. These culminated in a massive demonstration in Tiananmen Square in June, 1989. The tanks were quickly sent in and the army massacred the students. So as the decade was coming to an end, the Iron Curtain was coming down and democracy was rising in Eastern Europe. China begin to allow limited forms of capitalism, but the power and authority of the Communist Party would not be questioned or challenged. The Chinese saw the chaos that occurred when the Soviet Union collapsed and would not repeat their mistakes.

The mood in the U.S, and trust in government briefly rose in the early '90s as President Bush launched Operation Desert Storm to push Saddam Hussein's army out of Kuwait. He had miscalculated that the U.S. would look the other way when he grabbed the tiny oil-rich country. The American public supported the war and it generated a greater sense of national pride than during the controversial Vietnam War. But an uptick in unemployment in 1991 would cost President Bush a second term. He had seemed out of touch with the plight of the average American impacted by the economic downturn.

The "culture wars" over the social and political issues raised in the Awakening period were waged in the '90s between progressives and conservatives. The term was coined by James Davison Hunter in his 1991 book *The Culture Wars: The Struggle to Define America.* Battles were being fought in the courts, Congress, and for the White House to shift the balance of power deciding these emotionally charged issues: abortion, drug use, gun ownership, gay rights, religious rights, state's rights, and the role of government, among others. The culture wars were an understandable outcome of the social upheaval of the Awakening period. The status quo would predictably push back. The Unraveling of our social order would continue through the '90s.

Although Bill Clinton was elected President in 1992, the Republicans quickly took control of Congress in the 1994 mid-term elections for the first time since 1953, led by their "Contract with America" platform. President Clinton was impeached by the House of Representatives in November, 1998 but acquitted by the Senate in 1999, ending a bitter political battle over a sexual relationship Clinton had with an intern, Monika Lewinsky. Trust in government had been rising along with the economy in the '90s. But voter turnout had been declining steadily since 1968 as the electorate was becoming disenchanted with politics and government. Voter turnout hit 49% in 1996, the lowest since 1924, just before the Great Depression and when the last Crisis period began. Once again, the

Republicans were able to secure control of the government as the 'Silent Majority' voted while a majority in the country did not.

Figure 3-12.

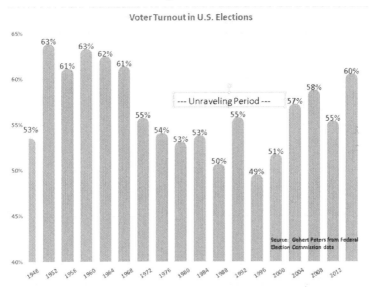

The conflict between political parties would escalate as the Unraveling period was drawing to a close. The controversial 2000 election between George W. Bush and Al Gore was too close to call for weeks due to the contested count in Florida, which was ultimately decided by the Supreme Court. Whoever won Florida, would win the election. That judicial decision exacerbated a deepening of the partisan divide between progressives and conservatives. Once again, low voter turnout benefitted the Republicans.

Figure 3-13.

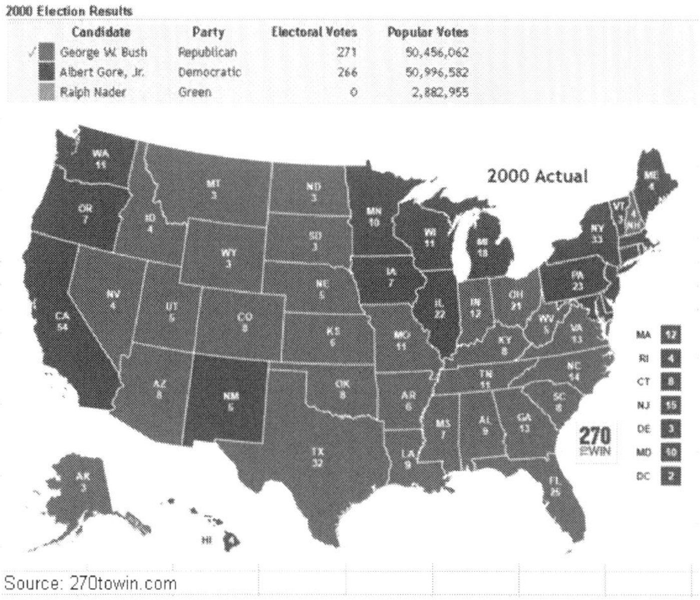

2000 Election Results

	Candidate	Party	Electoral Votes	Popular Votes
✓	George W. Bush	Republican	271	50,456,062
	Albert Gore, Jr.	Democratic	266	50,996,582
	Ralph Nader	Green	0	2,882,955

Source: 270towin.com

Economy

Reagan's economic policy message in 1980 called for a return to personal responsibility and family values. This message resonated with Americans frustrated by the decline in social order during the Awakening. He touted the virtue of supply-side economics, which advocated using incentives to stimulate the production of goods and services. Methods such as reducing income tax and capital-gains tax rates were advanced. Reagan promised drastic reduction in the size of government and a balanced budget. But the result of the tax cuts were larger budget deficits; his "trickle down" economics did little to support the middle class. The lead cohort of the Baby Boomers were turning 35 in 1980, and with millions more behind them, drove the economy with their heavy consumer

spending for the decade. Businesses were slashing costs
with restructuring and the U.S. surged ahead of Japan and
Europe in growth. Aside from the recessions in 1981 and
1983, GDP growth surged to over 3.5% but the federal
budget deficit soared to $150 billion, nearly triple the level
during the Carter years. The unemployment rate declined
steadily from a peak of nearly 11% in 1982 to 5% in 1989
as President Bush assumed office.

Figure 3-14.

The '80s would give rise to the digital age and the
rapid expansion of computers in business and government.
Increases in labor productivity would follow. Steve Jobs
and Apple would make this technology accessible for
everyone, with the creation of the personal computer.
The development of the World Wide Web was originally
started so researchers could communicate with each other
in the '80s but exploded in popularity for average users
with the development of convenient browsers in the '90s.
But as technology companies raced to get hardware and

software to the burgeoning business and consumer market, it was often with the encryption that was called "Pretty Good Privacy" or PGP. Cyber espionage and "hacking" would rise with the proliferation of computers. The ensuing conflict between government and the technology developers/users over data collection and encryption in pursuit of national security would follow.

A closer look at the overall growth in GDP would reveal that, starting in 1980, the income gap between rich and poor was widening and the middle class was falling behind. This point was made clearly in Mario Cuomo's "Two America's" speech at the Democratic National Convention in 1984. The top 5% were doing quite well while the rest made little progress. The gap would widen considerably as the decades continued. The gap would contribute to the negative social mood of the period.

Figure 3-15.

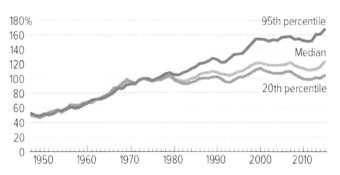

Income Gains Widely Shared in Early Postwar Decades — But Not Since Then

Real family income between 1947 and 2015, as a percentage of 1973 level

Note: In 2014 Census split its sample of survey respondents into two groups to test a set of redesigned income questions. In 2015 (reporting on 2014 income using the new questions), Census released two estimates of 2013 incomes: one based on the old questions and one on the new. The chart uses the estimate based on the old questions, based on CBPP's judgment that, due in part to sample size, it is likely more accurate for 2013.

Source: CBPP calculations based on U.S. Census Bureau Data

Trust in government dropped after the euphoria of victory in the first Gulf War wore off and unemployment rose in the early '90s. The recession in 1991 would limit President Bush to one term. Trust rose again throughout the '90s during the Clinton administration and while the Republicans controlled Congress - and the accompanying economic growth during the decade. Meanwhile, governmental regulation of Wall Street was relaxed with the philosophy that our economy would thrive with less oversight and regulation. Also during this time, the Savings and Loan Crisis (1986 – 95) resulted in the closure of nearly a third of all savings and loans across America. Poor management, deregulation, and high interest rates have all been cited as causes, but ultimately the cost borne by the taxpayer was over $120 billion.

Figure 3-16 Trust in Government

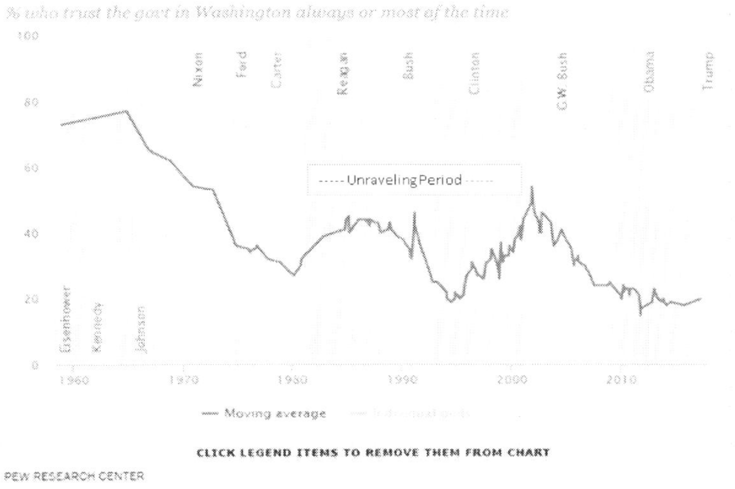

The Glass-Stegall Act had been put in place in 1933 as part of a major banking overhaul to prohibit commercial banks from making investment (speculation) activities that had caused the collapse of many banks. During the 1980s, the major provisions of this law were diluted to allow banks to own brokerage firms and mutual funds and act as both agent and principals in securities trading. The Democrats lost control of the Congress in 1994, just two years after Clinton took office. By 1999, the remaining provisions of Glass-Steagall had been repealed with Clinton's approval. That decision would be questioned after the financial meltdown in 2008. The lessons of the Savings & Loan crisis did not appear to have tempered the desire for greater deregulation.

In 1998 Commodity Futures Trading Commission (CFTC) chairperson Brooksley E. Born petitioned Congress and the President to give the CFTC oversight of "off-exchange markets" for over-the-counter (OTC) derivatives as well as its existing oversight of exchange-traded derivatives, but her warnings were strongly opposed by the powerful Federal Reserve Chairman Alan Greenspan, Treasury Secretaries Robert Rubin and Lawrence Summers as unnecessary and exaggerated. The consequences of this disregard for prudent regulation by leading government officials would be felt during the coming crisis period. Ms. Born was clear sighted in her concern for regulation of derivatives, while our regulators were woefully negligent and proven wrong.

As the '90s came to an end, concerns about Y2K and a tech bubble were widespread. An estimated $300 billion was spent to patch computers and applications nationwide to clean the suspected millennium bug. Dot-com companies with little sales and no profits were reaching valuations exceeding that of brick and mortar companies in the period between 1999 and 2000. The NASDAQ peaked at over 5,100 in March of 2000, but fell nearly 80% over the next two years. The rapacious spending to build to scale fast was typified by the 16 dot-com companies who spent millions advertising during Super Bowl XXXIV. Yet while many companies crashed and burned when the bubble burst, some companies, like Amazon and E-Bay, survived to forge a new millennium.

The Great Awakening set fire to many of the norms and values that had taken hold during the High period. These battles raged through the Unraveling period during the '80s and '90s. While the economy rose and unemployment fell in the '90s, the Unraveling period had seen a steady erosion in family structure, a divisive culture war between people and within our government, and a polarization in our media. The economy had progressed and benefited many, but as globalization increased, many others were left further behind. The national mood had declined steadily from the stable social order during the High period that had been built in the decades after WWII ended. How much worse could it get? As the millennium ended and President Bush settled into his first term in January 2001, we would soon find out.

Chapter 4
New American Crisis (2001 – 2017)

"The Fourth Turning is a Crisis, a decisive era of secular (social) upheaval, when the values regime propels the replacement of the old civic order with a new one."[35]

Figure 4-1.

				Social Behaviors and Attitudes					
Turning	Period	Families	Child Rearing	Gap in Gender Roles	Trust in Government	Voter Turnout	Social Priorities	New Gen Focus	Wars
Fourth Turning	Crisis	Strengthening	Over Protective	widening	increasing	increasing	rising community	fix outer world	decisive

The Unraveling period came to an abrupt and tragic end on September 11, 2001. Just as everyone alive in 1963 remembers exactly where they were on November 22, so too would they on that fateful morning. Other serious events during the 00s and the following decade would add to that underlying but persistent sense of crisis: the wars in Iraq and Afghanistan, the space shuttle Columbia disintegrating upon re-entry, climate change, Hurricane Katrina and the devastation in New Orleans, the financial crisis and Great Recession, mass shootings of children and others, political polarization in government and the news media, the rise of ISIS and terrorist attacks on soft civilian targets.

The Awakening period and Crisis periods are more significant (dominant) periods in social history than the (recessive) High and Unraveling periods. But just as 2,996 would sadly lose their lives that day, so too would a new generation (Gen Y) come of age and begin their lives as young adults. Every child born that day and until the crisis is resolved will carry the name of Gen Z. They would grow up in an era when terrorism, and the war to defeat it, was elevated to new heights. Heroes from all walks of life and fictional Superheroes would rise to new heights in popular culture.

Figure 4-2.

	Crisis Period 2002 - 2020			
	Children	Young Adults	Mid-Life Adults	Elders
Generation	Gen Z	Gen Y	Gen X	Baby Boomers
Archetype	Artist	Hero	Nomad	Prophet

The Hero archetype, increasingly protected as children, are perceived as good kids and empowered to make their mark on the world. They work together in a cooperative way to focus on building community, gaining influence, and advancing the technologies of their period.

Profile of Gen Y (Millennials)

Figure 4-3.   Figure 4-4.

"Generations, like people, have personalities, and Millennials have begun to forge theirs: confident, self-expressive, liberal, upbeat and open to change"[36]

according to a study by the Pew Research Center. They are more ethnically diverse, more educated and less religious than previous generations. Their embrace of technology will only be exceeded by Gen Z, who will be the first wholly 'digitally native' generation from birth. Pew goes on to report that the most important things to them are: "being a good parent, having a successful marriage, and helping others in need."[37] Having seen the impact of divorce on Gen X and their own generation as children, it is a natural desire to improve on whatever your parents may have done. At the same time, they have delayed getting married and having children, when compared with previous generations, perhaps in the hope of getting it right.

Like all generations before them, Millennials feel that they have a unique and distinctive identity. Their proficient and extensive use of technology in the daily pursuit of their lives is a key component of their group identity. They are more liberal than their Gen X predecessors in their acceptance of people of different ethnic groups and sexual orientation.

Gen Y's identity was forged in the events and circumstances of their childhood and youth. While every generation experiences tragic events during their early lives, the period in history and the accompanying mood has an impact on how those events are perceived. The U.S. had already undergone 20 years of divisive social turmoil by the time Millennials were first being born in 1981. The society would go through another 20 years of social unraveling, culture wars, and declining trust in government by the time they came of age, and the planes flew into the twin towers of the World Trade Center.

A wide range of events that occurred while Gen Y was growing up in the Unraveling period would shape their personal lives and the collective persona of the generation. Divorce had peaked at the start of their lives but remained high through their childhood. The Berlin Wall came down and the Soviet Union collapsed, but the risks of nuclear power became vivid with the reactor meltdown in Chernobyl in 1986. Terrorism was highlighted with the bombing of Pan Am #103 over Scotland in 1988 and the first bombings of the World Trade Center in 1993. Home-grown terrorists struck the Oklahoma City Federal building in 1995 and teenagers killed their classmates at Columbine High School in 1999. Many more shootings would follow. Personal computers emerged during their childhood and their relationship with the World Wide Web would deepen with the development of Netscape and other browsers to more easily surf the web. Globalization and the booming economy would benefit many but the gap between the middle class and the wealthy widened. The outside world was a very uncertain place and one that would need to be fixed.

The Baby Boomers had a very different childhood growing up in the stable, protected High period of 1945 to 1963. The destruction wrought by WWII was still very fresh in the minds of their elders, who made every effort to avoid another global crisis of that magnitude. But when the Boomers began to come of age after the Kennedy assassination, the time had come to overturn the conformist social norms that had persisted and advance the causes of disadvantaged groups that had been simmering. So the events that occurred are relevant but perceived within the context of the era itself. Millennials would respond in kind to the challenges that exist for their generation. And their place in the cycle has shaped their persona to meet their unique challenges.

Pop Culture

Like Baby Boomers, the Millennials have been studied and publicized far more than their predecessor, Gen X. Iconoculture Consumer Insights noted in a 2014 study titled "Millennial Ties that Bind"[38] that they reject any common portrayals, and as my eldest daughter always reminds me, but are tied together by events such as 9/11, the Second Gulf War, Social Media, and The Great Recession in short order. Iconoculture found the overlap between "cultural commonalities" and "core values" for Millennials in attributes such as flexibility, adaptability, uncertainty, and change. A Nielsen study in 2014 titled "Millennials – Breaking the Myth"[39] went further to say they are expressive, optimistic, struggling but entrepreneurial, desire authenticity, and want the personal touch. The digital age fused with smart phones in 2006, allowing consumers with immediate access to information. Since then, consumer product marketers have had to adjust both their message and the medium to communicate effectively and directly with Millennials.

Time Magazine christened them "The New Greatest Generation" in its May, 2013 cover issue. While Gen Y is dramatically reshaping the economy and social order, that moniker feels like hyperbole as of yet. The crisis period they would help to overcome would not approach the magnitude of the global devastation of the Great Depression and WWII, but not all crises are created equal. But the need for courage, optimism, and cooperation is the same. The challenges of the on-going war on terror, a dysfunctional government, and lack of public trust in institutions must all be overcome before we can breathe in the fresh spring air of a new High period.

As Millennials entered their teen years in the mid-to late '90s, Hollywood provided them films that would give us a glimpse of their emerging identity. The theme of the 2001 movie *Pearl Harbor* called for heroism and collective action, a far cry from that of *American Beauty,* which was nominated for eight Academy Awards in 2000 and could be described as a sad depiction of how the Unraveling had misshaped family life in America. *Ed TV* and the *Truman Show* were both early versions of reality TV that would dominate the 00s, but also look remarkably like the first "selfies." But every generation takes its own version of a Hero's journey and films like *Harry Potter, The Matrix,* and *Lord of the Rings* have provided the backdrop for that metaphor for Millennials. The events that occurred during the Unraveling period coincided with the childhood and youth of the Millennials. As disruptive as those were, events took a turn for the worse as they began to turn 20 in 2001. After 9/11, heroes needed to have greater powers and do even greater things. *The Dark Knight*, *Spiderman,* and the *Hunger Games* raised the stakes. There have been six releases of *Spiderman* since the Crisis period began. Young Gen Z is absorbing all of this hero culture and it is shaping their collective persona as well.

As the crisis period progressed, with Millennials actively delaying marriage and having children, film took a lighter view of growing older with *Wedding Crashers*, *Bridesmaids*, *The Hangover*, *Juno* and *Knocked Up.* Will Smith made learning the skills needed to secure a relationship with a woman seem easy in *Hatch* in 2006. Since many Millennials had to actually seek refuge back in their parents' homes due to high student debt and stalled careers, *Failure to Launch* struck a familiar chord that captured a unique experience for their generation. The Great Recession soon followed and made matters even worse for many. The median age for a first marriage jumped to over 28 for men by 2010.

Figure 4-5.

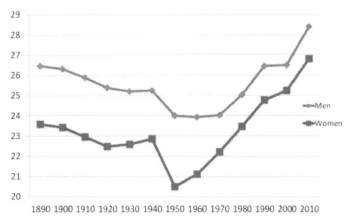

Figure 1. Median Age at First Marriage by Sex: 1890 to 2010

John Mayer expressed Gen Y's reluctance and fear of growing older in his 2006 hit song, Stop This Train.

But grow up they will. The teamwork, optimism, and adaptability that Gen Y portrays will play a greater role each year in creating a more stable and effective social order. They are moving into more responsible roles in business as well as starting families at home. Home buying is on the uptick and upcoming elections in 2018 will see Millennials having a much greater impact on the outcome.

Women and Family

Issues related to women and family had surfaced during the Awakening period in the '60s. Abortion and divorce increased rapidly, would peak during the Unraveling period and then decline through the Crisis period. After rising rapidly after the passage of Roe v. Wade in 1973, the abortion rate peaked in 1980 at 29.3 per 1000 women of childbearing age and has fallen steadily ever since. The greater availability, efficacy and use of contraceptives has had a positive impact on this trend. Nearly half (45%) of all pregnancies in 2011 were unintended, but only four in 10 of these were terminated. More than half of all abortion patients were in their twenties, with most of those 24 and younger.

Figure 4-6.

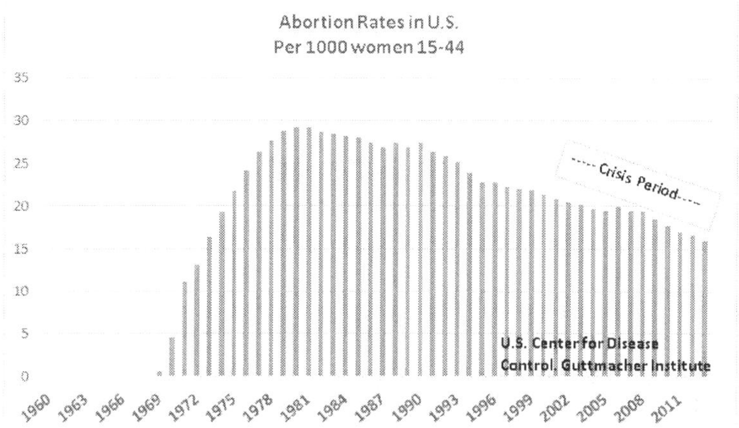

Abortion Rates in U.S.
Per 1000 women 15-44

Crisis Period

U.S. Center for Disease Control, Guttmacher Institute

Important for policy makers to consider is that 75% of all abortion patients were low-income or poverty level. A Guttmacher Institute survey captured the major reasons cited by patients for having an abortion; existing responsibility for others, inability to afford raising a child, and the belief that having a child would interfere with work, school, or the ability to care for other dependents. According to the Guttmacher Institute (GPR Policy Review 2016, Vo. 19), the 13% decline in abortions between 2008 and 2011 was driven by a steep drop in unintended pregnancy, which they attributed to the greater use of contraceptives. They maintain that supporting and expanding women's access to contraceptive services leads to a lower incidence of abortion.

The fertility rate dropped to 1.9 births per woman in 2010. That is below the 2.1 births per woman needed to sustain the population. The birth rate (births per 1000 population) had been declining since 1990 and plunged further after the Great Recession struck in 2007. Teenage births have dropped steadily since 1990, while births to older women (35-39) and (40-44) have been rising steadily. Meanwhile, births to younger women (20-29) have been declining. Women are waiting longer to have children, consistent with the delay in getting married. Births to unmarried women continues to average over 40% of all births. Among Hispanic and white women, 68% of all non-marital births occurred within cohabitation living arrangements.

Figure 4-7.

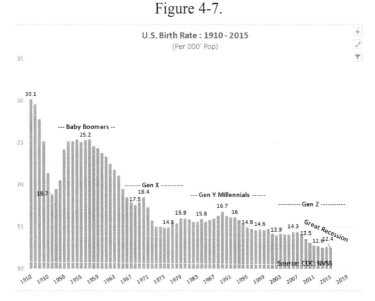

Divorce rates rose rapidly from 1963 to 1980. They remained at that level for the next twenty years and then began a steady descent between 2000 and 2010. Divorce rates are only 10% for couples with a college degree but nearly 20% for those with only some college or those with only a high school education or less.

Figure 4-8.

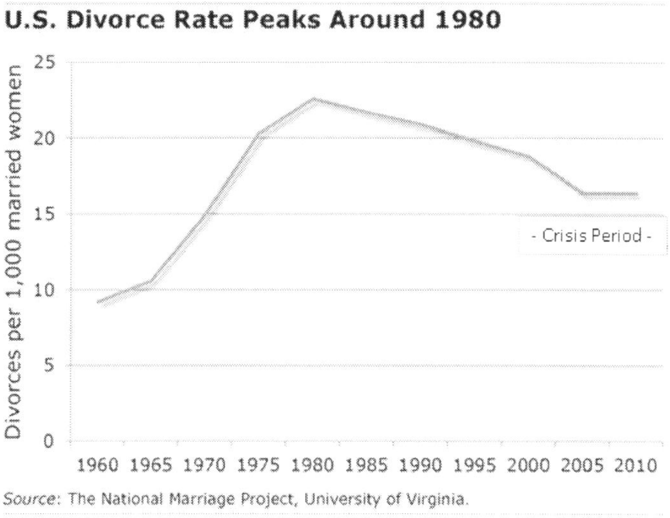

U.S. Divorce Rate Peaks Around 1980

Source: The National Marriage Project, University of Virginia.

The decline in divorce coincides with a continued decline in marriages, which have plunged from 10.6 per 1000 population in 1980 to 6.8 per 1000 in 2015. The problem is more acute at lower income and education levels. Millennials have not yet embraced the traditional structure of marriage or having children. This may be an understandable reaction to seeing the frequency of failed marriages of the generations before them and the resulting impact on themselves and the generation before them. Like other changes Gen Y is driving, they may well be in the process of reinventing marriage and child-rearing. The family structure has shifted from the traditional nuclear family in the 1950's to a variety of blended families. Some homes have a single head of the home, some a married man and women, some simply cohabitating men and women, some headed by gay couples of either gender. The families are made up of children from previous relationships as well as the current relationships.

Figure 4-9.

With the decline in marriage rates, only 32% of 18-34 year olds are married compared with 62% in 1960. Living arrangements also have shifted in conjunction with the decline in marriages. More people are living alone (14%) or living with parents (32%). Once again, those without a college degree have a higher incidence of living at home (36%) versus those with a college degree (19%). Prior to the start of the crisis period, Gen X-ers had begun getting married and having children. As a natural reaction to the under-protective childhood they had as children, their parenting style naturally shifted to the opposite. The cover of Time magazine in November 2009 appealed for "The Case Against Over-Parenting." Their tendency to be over-protective out of a desire to give their children the security and stability they lacked will imbue many in that new generation with the risk-adverse, conforming personality that we have seen before in the Silent generation. In a 2015 Pew Research Center survey, 68% of Millennials say they are sometimes "over-protective" compared to 60% for Gen X and 54% for Baby Boomers. In addition, 40% of Millennials say they praise too much, higher than for other generations.

With all of the turmoil that many American families have undergone since the 1960's, the desire for a shift back to a more tranquil time is understandable. The *Wall Street Journal* reported on June 13, 2015 on *Television Habits That Put Family First* that recent colorized reruns of *I Love Lucy* drew an average of 6.4 million viewers, nearly twice as many who watched the recent finale of Mad Men. It cited a study published in the Journal of Adolescent Research in 2014, which found positive outcomes for families that made time for shared activities like watching television or on the internet. Some families in the study also indicated a desire for "safe" shows to watch like "*Mayberry RFD*" and "*The Andy Griffith Show,*" classic family shows in the last High period.

Crime and Gun Violence

Crime rates show an interesting pattern for the periods of the cycle. Data is available for the murder rate all the way back to 1900. The murder rate began rising rapidly during an earlier Awakening period which ended in 1908 and accelerated during the subsequent Unraveling period. It tracked down steadily though the Crisis and High period until 1960. As in the last cycle, the murder rate began rising rapidly during the latest Awakening period (1960s) and stayed high through the recent Unraveling period. The descent began in 1991 and has continued through the crisis period based on data available through 2015. Murder rates are, in fact, at a 60-year low. This is in contrast to the unique situation occurring in Chicago where murder rates have sky-rocketed due to inter-gang turf wars and the wave of mass shootings that have occurred over the past twenty years.

Figure 4-10.

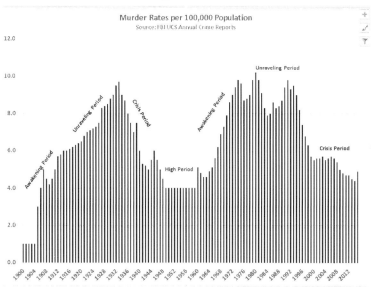

The total crime rate shows a similar pattern, but reliable data for property crimes is either not readily available or comparable prior to 1958. What we can see is that, like the murder rate, total crime (property and violent) rose steadily during the Awakening period from 1963 to 1980. It remained high but leveled off during the Unraveling period and began a steady downward trend in 1991, which has continued through the Crisis period through data for 2015.

Figure 4-11.

Total Crime in U.S. - Property and Violent
(Rate per 000 Pop)

The on-going debate over the rights afforded our citizens under the Second Amendment would galvanize Americans during the new millennium with numerous and tragic multiple homicides. A mentally ill student at Virginia Tech was allowed to purchase guns in spite of his diagnosis, since he was not institutionalized. He murdered 32 people on the campus in a shooting rampage in April, 2007 before committing suicide. The public outrage resulted in the strengthening of the laws in Virginia as well as in the National Instant Criminal Background Check System with President Bush's approval. But the killings continued. A student with mental-health issues killed five and injured 21 in an attack at Northern Illinois University the following year. In 2011, U.S. Rep. Gaby Gifford was seriously wounded in an assassination attempt that killed six by a man with mental-health issues. And in 2012, a lone gunman dressed in camo gear and armed with automatic weapons killed 12 and injured 58 at a movie theater in Aurora, less than 20 miles from where two students killed 13 and injured 21 at Columbine high school during the childhood of the Millennial generation. But nothing could prepare the nation for the unspeakable horror that would occur in December 2012 with the senseless murder of twenty young children and eight adults at Sandy Hook Elementary school by a former student with obsessive-compulsive disorder (OCD) as well as Asperger syndrome. In spite of these tragic events, no other action was taken to tighten gun laws and the country remains deeply divided over the issue.

A Pew Research Center study completed in August, 2016 showed bi-partisan support among voters for several gun-policy proposals, including: background checks for private and gun-show sales, preventing people with mental illness from purchasing guns, and banning gun purchases by people on the federal no-fly list. In comparison, support diverged significantly on proposals for creating a federal database to track gun sales, a ban on high capacity ammunition clips, and a ban on assault-style weapons. A related survey shows that the overall support to control gun ownership has declined from 2007 to 2015, in spite of the many mass shootings that occurred over that period.

Climate Change

Social attitudes regarding climate change have risen along with the scientific evidence presented. The concerns over climate change, global warming, and the level of CO_2 gases had been rising in the public arena since 1965, when a President's Advisory Commission warned that it was a very real issue. Even conservative British Prime Minister Margaret Thatcher called for an international treaty on climate change in 1989. So when President Bush formally removed the United States from the Kyoto Protocol process in 2001, the national debate accelerated. But the Atlantic hurricane season of 2004 provided a more urgent and tangible narrative when four severe hurricanes struck Florida, killing over 100 people and causing over $50B in damage. The acrimonious debate continued and the 2005 season bought a deadly trio of hurricanes, but nothing compared with the Category 3 Hurricane Katrina that devastated the Gulf coast and New Orleans. The failure of the local, state, and federal governments to provide timely and effective relief to those stranded in the aftermath would further amplify the feeling of a loss of trust in our country's institutions.

Weather events resulting in the loss of life and billions of dollars in property damage would continue to punctuate the crisis period. The political divide within the country over the issue would persist in spite of graphic images of receding polar ice caps and glaciers and documented rising world temperatures. The ensuing years would see Hurricane Ike in 2008 and massive tornadoes in the heartland in 2008, 2011 and again in 2013. President Obama would agree to the historic Paris Treaty in 2015, only to see President Trump pull out of it in June, 2017. Hurricane Harvey would completely inundate the Texas coast with rain over three days and flood Houston and Corpus Christi in August.

The Unraveling and Crisis periods have seen a widening of opinions between the public and scientists. The result has been greater polarization around policy issues that involve scientific evidence. A Pew Research Center study conducted in 2014 showed a wide gap between the percentage of agreement by the public and of scientists on several major topics; safe to eat genetically modified food (51), safe to eat foods grown with pesticides (40), humans have evolved over time (33), and climate change is mostly due to human activity (37). Although Americans broadly support the crucial role of science, they diverge when it comes to implications for policy decisions. As a result, climate change and other scientifically based events continue to be a point of polarization during the current crisis period.

Foreign Policy

The terrorist attacks on 9/11 resulted in the passage of the Patriot Act in 2001. The law provided government with expanded rights of surveillance, detention, and punishment for persons convicted of acts of terrorism, conspiracy or aiding and abetting. The following year, the Department of Homeland Security was established to provide a centralized structure for combatting all forms of crimes against the United States. After the surprise attack on Pearl Harbor in the last crisis period, the government had similar leeway to reduce individual freedoms in the name of national security when they established internment camps for U.S. citizens of Japanese descent. The national good supersedes the individual good during a crisis period.

The country was galvanized to a common purpose and, more importantly, a common national identity under "United We Stand." That would come to include "Boston Strong" after the bombings at the Boston Marathon in April, 2013. This was a time where heroes and heroism were called for. After a short period when people struggled to understand "why do they hate us?" President Bush provided the explanation that most nations use in a time of war, it was a fight between "good and evil." Our national will power was summoned and action was swift. Someone had awakened the sleeping giant. The U.S. was firmly in the middle of an "extroverted" foreign policy mood and the coming decades would see assertive military action, with national security as the foundational rationale.

Figure 4-12.

Theory of Cycles	1980	1985	1990	1995	2000	2005	2010	2015
Strauss & Howe - Generational Cycles								
High								
Awakening								
Unraveling		Unraveling						
Crisis						Crisis		
Schlesinger - Political								
Public Purpose				Public				
Private interest	Private						Private	
Klingberg - Foreign Policy								
Extrovert				Extrovert				
Introvert								

It was quickly apparent that the 9/11 attacks were orchestrated by Osama bin Laden, a Saudi from a wealthy family turned radical Islamic jihadist and leader of Al-Qaeda. He had been living and operating his jihadist organization out of Afghanistan, which was controlled by the Taliban, a conservative Islamist group that had prevailed in the Afghan civil war following the defeat of the Soviet army. The Taliban predictably rejected our demands that bin Laden be handed over, consistent with their own religious sentiments, as well as in keeping with the traditional Afghan practice of "Pashtunwali," where even enemies are provided safekeeping once harbored. In response, the U.S. launched Operation Enduring Freedom on October 7, 2001.

Like the Russians and the British before them, we would become embroiled in Afghanistan, which had learned over the centuries how to artfully function as a buffer state between competing empires. Afghanistan is a poor landlocked country that navigated their autonomy while the Persian, Russian and British empires surrounded them. The full story of this stretches back 500 years to the time of Ivan the Great (1480) and is richly told in

Peter Hopkirk's seminal book *The Great Game,* published in 1990. Rather than plunging headlong into a military invasion of Afghanistan, as the Russians regretfully did in 1979, we skillfully waged a proxy war using regional warlords and their militias, C.I.A. operatives, Special Forces, and targeted airpower. We quickly overthrew the Taliban and sent bin Laden into hiding in a labyrinth of caves in the Hindu Kush mountain range that bordered Pakistan. A pro-western government headed by Hamid Karzai was established following a national assembly (loya jirja) and presidential elections. The Taliban viewed Karzai simply as a U.S. puppet even though he was an ethnic Pashtun like themselves.

When the news media reports that we have been fighting in Afghanistan for 16 years and it has been our longest war, they usually fail to add that the Bush administration only sent about 20,000 U.S. troops to the country from 9/11 through 2007, with the focus on Special Forces. We had quickly shifted direction and scaled up to over 140,000 troops in Iraq after the invasion in 2003. Afghanistan was no longer a priority. It was not until 2010 that Obama sent a sizeable combat force to Afghanistan in respond to the falling security situation there.

Figure 4-13.

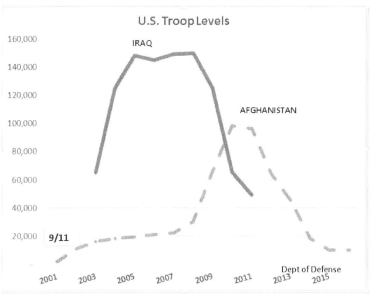

The Taliban mounted an effective counter offensive and re-established control over many regions, which they have used to undermine first the Karzai government and the current Ghani government. President Obama sent the first sizable force in 2009-2013 which improved security, but he quickly tapered troop levels down during his re-election campaign in 2012, and has since reduced the troop levels to 9,800 in 2015 as he prepared to leave office. The conflict has dragged on for seventeen years due to vacillating U.S. policy, while neither a political solution nor a military victory has yet been achieved. The Afghan National Army is more proficient than before, but the Taliban has made inroads since U.S. troop levels were reduced. They continue to launch terrorist attacks on government and civilian targets in major cities. Osama bin Laden was killed in Pakistan in 2011, but the Pakistani government continues to harbor Taliban leaders near the border. Without either an effective political settlement or a military victory over the Taliban, security in Afghanistan will remain elusive which affects securityin the surrounding region.

Figure 4-14.

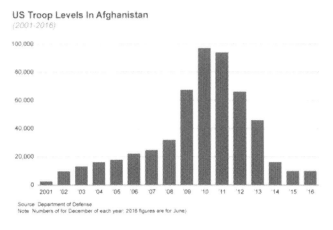

US Troop Levels In Afghanistan
(2001-2016)

Source: Department of Defense
Note: Numbers of for December of each year: 2016 figures are for June)

Our leaders' attention had shifted to Iraq, the oil-rich area to the west of Afghanistan. At a time when the public would support the government in dealing with nearly any threat to the homeland, the intelligences services reported to Bush and his policy makers that Saddam Hussein still had weapons of mass destruction (WMD's), and that he or his proxy might use those against our country. The U.S. Congress voted in favor of the use of force in a resolution enacted Oct. 16, 2002. After Secretary of State Colin Powell's emphatic presentation on the presence of WMD's in Iraq at the UN on Feb. 5, 2003, the U.S. moved swiftly to act, in spite of the fact that a majority of Americans were in favor of a diplomatic solution. While the U.K., Australia, and Poland joined the coalition in the attack on Iraq, France and Germany were strongly opposed, as was most of the Muslim world. Operation Iraqi Freedom was launched in

March, 2003 and quickly deposed the Baathist government of Saddam Hussein.

Although President Bush celebrated "Mission Accomplished" for the quick military victory our troops achieved, the war was far from over. The premise for the war would quickly unravel, as would the social order that Saddam's brutal dictatorship had enforced over twenty-four years. The (Sunni) Saudi government had implored President Bush's father not to topple Saddam during the first Gulf war in 1991. They feared the rise of Iranian influence in the largely Shiite country. He wisely followed that advice. The security situation in Iraq only got worse after the fall of Hussein. The decisions by the Bush administration to outlaw the ruling Sunni Ba'ath party, and push members of the party out of a working government, along with the decision to disband the Iraqi army, quickened the fall into a bloody civil war from 2006 to 2008. One that would cost many American lives as well.

Figure 4-15.

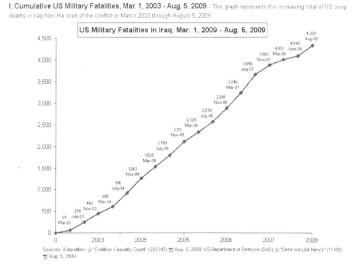

I. Cumulative US Military Fatalities, Mar. 1, 2003 - Aug. 5, 2009 - This graph represents the increasing total of US troop deaths in Iraq from the start of the conflict in March 2003 through August 5, 2009.

Sources: iCasualties ☆ "Coalition Casualty Count" (225 KB) 🎮 Aug. 5, 2009; US Department of Defense (DoD) ☆ "Defense Link News" (11 KB); 🎮 Aug. 5, 2009

The mood and attitudes in the U.S. would devolve as well, when it became clear that there was a massive "intelligence failure" that led to the war. Many in the country believed that the administration encouraged the conclusions they received from the intelligence community, and tacitly discouraged the advancement of other conclusions. The CIA and entire intelligence community is within the executive branch of government, so careers were at stake. The war on terror was not over, but the unity of the country was torn and frayed by the false premise of a costly and on-going war. The situation in Afghanistan deteriorated as well, only adding to the on-going crisis mood in the country. Abu Ghraib prison, Guantanamo, and "renditions" would contribute to the decline of our global prestige. The public trust in government continued to fade as the Crisis period progressed.

Figure 4-16 Trust in Government

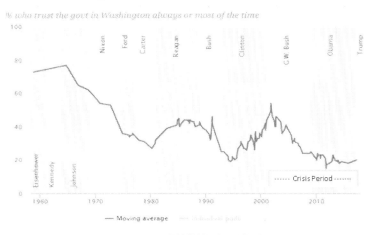

Al Qaeda took political control of Anbar province in the west. President Bush ordered a "surge" of over 20,000

troops in 2007 to establish the security needed for the Iraqis to govern and protect themselves. The sale of advanced weapon systems to Iraq would follow. The strategy was successful and helped the Shiite government establish control over the country. Bush negotiated a timetable for withdrawing U.S. troops from Iraq and signed the Status of Forces Agreement in 2008 that stipulated all U.S. military forces would leave Iraq by December, 2011. President Obama made no effort to modify that agreement. Obama reduced the combat troop levels during 2009 – 2011 and pulled all of them out in 2012. While President Obama's decision to leave Iraq without leaving a force protection (counter terrorism) contingent behind was ill-advised, the presence of the U.S. military would only delay inevitable sectarian conflict without meaningful inclusion of the Sunnis in the national government. Prime Minister Nouri al-Maliki of Iraq had no such intention.

But trouble was also brewing in neighboring Syria and throughout the region. The Arab Spring started after the self-immolation of a Tunisian street vendor in 2010 as a protest against the endemic harassment and extortion of merchants by city officials in 2011. This ignited a wave of protests in Tunisia and other countries across the region for better government. The Egyptian government of Hosni Mubarak was toppled and he would be put on trial. In February of 2011 Libya was experiencing a well-organized uprising by a cross-section of military and political figures aligned against Gaddafi's regime. They formed the National Transitional Council (NTC) as a ruling body. Gaddafi responded with counter-attacks and civilian atrocities ensued. After a Security Council Resolution to protect civilians, NATO responded with bombings which helped the NTC defeat Gaddafi and his loyalists. He was captured and executed by the rebels. An Islamist militia attacked the U.S. Consulate in Benghazi on September

11, 2012 and killed Ambassador Christopher Stevens and three others. Secretary of State Clinton was assailed for a lack of protection for the Consulate and an inaccurate and poorly constructed narrative on the cause of the attack. ISIS affiliates murdered Christians throughout Libya as well. The Libyan civil war that followed the fall of Gaddafi mirrored the aftermath of the invasion of Iraq and the fall of Saddam Hussein. President Obama had learned a vivid lesson about military interventions in the Middle East that would influence his decision to minimize any involvement in Syria.

The President of Syria, Bashar al-Assad, took note of the deposed leaders of Libya and Egypt and potential implications for himself and responded with brutal force to suppress the protests in his country that occurred after the Arab Spring. Blaming foreigners for the uprising, the army massacred civilians in multiple cities. As President Obama was re-elected for his second term in 2012, we had pulled out of Iraq and were quickly scaling down troop levels in Afghanistan. The civil war in Syria was under way. President Obama had no intention of becoming embroiled in another war in the Middle East and most Americans had little appetite for it as well. President Obama would focus his foreign policy in troubled areas more on the increased use of drones, a joint cyber-attack on Iranian centrifuges with Israel, and political negotiations.

ISIS rose to prominence in Iraq and Syria due to the long-standing religious conflict between Shiite and Sunni Muslims that extends back to the time of the prophet Mohammed's death, marked by their divergent viewpoints on who was appropriate to succeed him and what form the Islamic religious dogma should take. (Sunni and Shiite are both sects of Islam, similar to how Catholic and Protestant are both sects of Christianity, which also experienced many bloody conflicts between them.) The subsequent triggering events for the rise of ISIS in each country were unmet demands for better representation within the country by Sunni Muslims, which were either ignored (Iraq) or violently suppressed (Syria) by the government. ISIS achieved military victories and territorial control first in Syria following Alawite (Shiite) President Assad's brutal repression of the majority Sunni and minority Kurd's protests for better governance in March 2011, inspired by the Arab Spring in other Mideast countries. Like Iraq, Syria had been ruled by a minority party, but in this case it was Assad's Shia rule over the majority Sunni's.

President Obama took a passive approach to the conflict and refused to provide any substantive military aid to the various anti-Assad elements. His failure to strike Assad in 2013 after chemical weapons were used in violation of his "red-line" weakened the U.S. standing in the region and the position of the rebels. Obama's negotiations with Syria's ally Iran for a nuclear agreement were on-going at the time and the larger goal was securing a freeze on nuclear weapons development. The bargain he struck with Assad that Syria would turn over all his chemical weapons to the Russians in lieu of U.S. military action, was discredited when Assad subsequently used chemical weapons against civilians in rebel-held areas. The Russians and Iranian-backed militias in Lebanon were more than prepared to support their long-time ally Assad in suppressing the anti-government forces and help secure his hold on power.

The conditions for sectarian conflict in Iraq had been created after the U.S.-led invasion of Iraq in 2003 and the subsequent fall of Saddam Hussein. Saddam Hussein, a Sunni, had ruled the Shiite majority country for decades with the help of the army and brutal security forces. Iraq is the only ethnic Arab country with a Shiite majority. Iran, where over 60% of the people are ethnic Persian, is also a

Shiite country. The largely Sunni Iraqi army was disbanded and the (Sunni) Baath party was outlawed by the Coalition Provisional Authority, headed by President Bush's special envoy, L. Paul Bremer, who reported directly to President Bush. This left the Sunni's with no vehicle for effective representation, or protection, in the new Iraq. Sunni militias were formed and civil war was under way soon after victory was declared by President Bush. It would take many American lives and billions of dollars before a fragile peace was established.

By 2014, ISIS had quickly spread from Syria to Iraq with little resistance from the Shiite-dominated Iraqi army or the Sunni locals, who had no practical alternative. The Saudi warning to President George H.W. Bush to leave Saddam Hussein in power following the first Iraq war was now clearly understood. Shite Iraq was now more closely aligned with Shite Iran and the Sunni areas were under the control of the radical Sunni group ISIS, similar to the Sunni Al-Qaeda group which had attacked the U.S. on 9/11. By 2017, ISIS control of Syria and Iraq was substantially reduced. They have been squeezed from all four sides: by Assad and his allies Russia from the West, by Iran and the Kurds from the east, by Turkey from the north and by the Iraqi army from the south. The U.S. has been supporting the Iraqi army and the Kurds.

Against the backdrop of the fight against ISIS are the 400,000 people who have died in the Syrian civil war, including 100,000 civilians according to the United Nations and Arab League. Then there are the nearly 5 million refugees who have fled Syria for Turkey, Jordan, Lebanon, Iraq, the EU and elsewhere. ISIS has responded to the loss of the caliphate by encouraging attacks on soft civilian targets in the Middle East, Europe, and the U.S. Terrorism as a mode of warfare was resurgent globally and the tactics would morph as conditions changed. More soft targets were chosen with weapons of opportunity, like cars or trucks running over pedestrians. Defeating terrorism ultimately requires providing a genuine social and political alternative to its ideology, along with the military capability to defend it.

The American people understand that a radical Islamist caliphate across Syria and Iraq is a real threat to the region as well as to the U.S. itself. The sanctuary provided to Al-Qaeda in Afghanistan made that abundantly clear. We are in a global war with an ideology as dangerous as Fascism and Communism, an ideology that is fundamentally incompatible with western democracy. But Americans are also very wary of military interventions in Muslim countries after the costly and questionable war in Iraq and our nearly twenty-year involvement in Afghanistan. Terrorism and the wars in the Middle East had become a central part of the Crisis period, but eroded rather than improved trust in government. But the soldiers that served were rightfully treated as heroes.

Economy

The Crisis escalated in 2007 with the burst of the housing bubble that had been building for over five years. Compounding the problem of the bubble itself, was the massive amounts of sub-prime (toxic) loans that were bundled and sold worldwide to unsuspecting buyers. These loans originated with U.S. banks and were securitized into collateral debt obligations (CDO's) and sold off domestically and abroad. The ensuing collapse of the housing market triggered a cascade of bankruptcies across the financial sector. The economy plunged into the worst recession since the Great Depression, with large financial institutions precipitating the crisis without proper oversight by government. Unemployment rose rapidly to 10% in

2009 and millions of people lost their homes. Economic turmoil would now add to the 9/11 terrorist attacks, multiple wars in the Middle East, political polarization in Congress, and an unraveling social fabric to create a deepening crisis mood.

Figure 4-17.

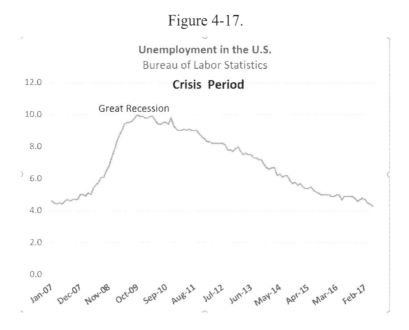

President Bush's Presidency (2001 – 2009) was bracketed by the 9/11terrorist attacks in his first year and the start of the Great Recession near his last, with the Iraq War in between. President Bush responded with $700 billion to purchase troubled mortgage assets (TARP) and prop up the banks. Interest rates were reduced throughout 2008. By January, 2009, as the economy plunged into the recession, the Democrats and Barak Obama took control of the government. It would be the worst recession since the Great Depression which occurred during the last Crisis period. The Democrats responded with an $800 billion stimulus program reminiscent of FDR's New Deal policy initiatives. A bailout of the auto industry followed. The Crisis period witnessed lower GDP growth rates than prior periods in the cycle and a painful recession. The impact would be felt by all generations at different stages of their lives; Baby Boomers as they were retiring, Gen X as they stepped into mid-life, and Gen Y as they moved into the young-adult stage.

Figure 4-18.

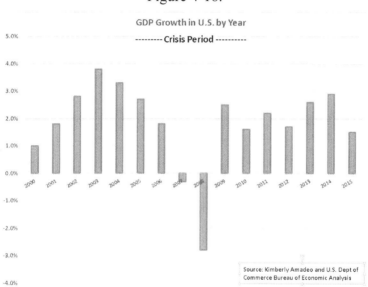

Political

After nearly 12 years of Republican control of the Congress and 8 years in the White House, the country was ready for a change. Public trust in government had plunged since its peak in 2001, when the country was briefly united behind President Bush after 9/11. The grinding war in Iraq and the lack of any WMD's had sapped the administration of public support and trust in government. The Iraq war also frayed our relations with key European allies and diluted global political support for the U.S., which was unquestionable immediately after the attacks on 9/11. Much of this trust had dissipated with the realization of the fallacious assumptions for the war in Iraq.

Figure 4-19 Trust in Government

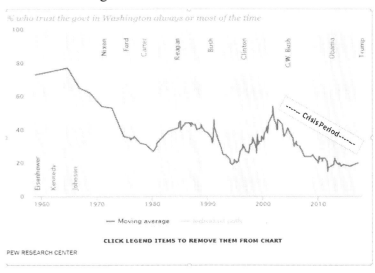

Barak Obama emerged as the Democratic nominee after defeating Hillary Clinton in the primaries in 2008. The United States would have an African-American President before it would have a woman president. He went on to win a landslide victory over John McCain in the general election and the Democrats took control of the House and Senate in January, 2009 for the first time since 1995. In addition to dealing with a plunging economy described above, President Obama and the Democratic Congress worked on health-care legislation without any Republican involvement over the next 14 months and in March, 2010 enacted the Affordable Care Act (Obamacare). The Republicans clamored against the "government take-over of health care." The Democrats paid quickly and dearly for their unilateral way of running the government. When the mid-term elections were held in 2010, they lost control of the House by a decisive margin, with 64 seats swinging to Republicans. The Senate would follow in 2014. With the House securely in the hands of Republicans and the Democrats controlling the Senate and White House, all progress in government was effectively halted and the tone deteriorated rapidly. In this crisis period, unlike the previous one (1929-1945), a dysfunctional government would be an integral part of the turmoil and negative mood.

Figure 4-20.

	Senate				
	2008	2010	2012	2014	2016
Democrats	57	51	53	44	46
Republicans	41	47	45	54	52
Independents	2	2	2	2	2

	House				
	2008	2010	2012	2014	2016
Democrats	257	193	201	188	194
Republicans	178	242	233	247	241

The polarization between political parties has its roots in widely divergent views on the size, scope, and role of government. This is a debate that has been waged since the founding of the nation. In a November, 2015 study released by the Pew Research Center, there was bipartisan support for government involvement in six major areas; ensuring national security, responding to natural disasters, ensuring safe food and medicine, managing immigration, maintaining infrastructure, and even advancing space exploration. The Pew Research study noted wide partisan disagreement on the need for government involvement in protecting the environment, strengthening the economy, ensuring access to education, ensuring access to health care, and helping people out of poverty. The basis of this disagreement on policy issues relates to philosophical differences over the efficacy of government as well as the view that the private sector (business and individuals) should handle those issues.

The economy slowly but steadily recovered from the Great Recession with unemployment dropping from 10% in 2009 to 4.3% in 2017. The deepest recession since the Great Depression would have the slowest recovery since then as well. The stock market, home to America's 401k savings, reached a new record in 2016 and again in 2017. But the political mood remained in crisis mode with greater polarization between the parties and a lack of any meaningful cooperation...on anything. That polarization accelerated in 2015-16 with the start of the presidential campaign. While Hillary Clinton received the nomination of the Democratic Party, populist Bernie Sanders generated a broad, vocal enthusiasm throughout his campaign. The Republican Party experienced an all-out civil war for control of the party. Out of a pack of 16 mostly conservative Republican candidates, Donald Trump defied all odds and secured the nomination. The tone and rhetoric of the campaign could easily be characterized as unprecedented in modern history. This was a foreshadowing of how toxic the general election campaign would be.

Trump resurrected Reagan's campaign slogan from 1980, with the slightly abbreviated "Make America Great Again." He carried a full-throated populist message to America's forgotten white middle class that harkened back to the better days of the American High in the 1950s. While segments of the electorate have moved across party lines before, this time it occurred in midst of a crisis period.

Trump skillfully ran a focused campaign that would give him narrow victories (total of 107,000 votes) in three key northern states (Pennsylvania, Michigan and Wisconsin), but a lopsided electoral victory. Even had Clinton won those three key states, she still would have been two electoral votes short of the 270 required to win. But Hillary Clinton won the popular vote by 2.9 million votes, with large victories in traditional Democratic states. After a long negative campaign, and with Trump dismissing his huge loss in the popular vote with unsubstantiated and widely repudiated claims of massive voter fraud, the divisive mood would continue. The country was as divided as the vote count.

Chapter 5
Crisis Resolution (2017 – 2020)

The 2016 presidential election only served to escalate the crisis mood in America. Regardless of which candidate had won the election, the crisis mood was going to continue as both candidates were deeply unpopular with half of the country. Since President Trump took office in January, 2017 several issues have dominated the public's attention: Trump's tweets and overall behavior, his executive order to ban entry to U.S. by people from selected Muslim countries, repeal and replacement of Obamacare, Russian interference in the 2016 Presidential election, and his conflict with the (liberal) media and repeated claims of "fake news."

In the context of cycles and generations, the Baby Boomers should have stepped aside to create an opportunity for Gen X candidates from both parties who could offer what the country needed – generational change! The Democrats had eight years to identify and prepare young candidates to replace Obama. But Hillary Clinton was determined to be the Democratic nominee after losing to Obama in 2000. The issue was not whether she was qualified or could garner significant votes from her core Democratic constituency, but that she was a polarizing figure to all Republicans and many Independents. Clinton, like Trump, would also not have been able to heal the national divide and her presidency would have been saddled with partisan investigations into her past. Her use of a private server in her basement and doubts about providing adequate protection for the Benghazi Consulate eroded trust in her by many, who did also not want to see another Bush or Clinton in the White House. But for the 66 million people who voted for Hillary Clinton, the political crisis had clearly worsened. Trump was as controversial and unpopular as she was with many.

The divisive nature and rhetoric of the Republican primaries and the presidential campaign itself served only to reinforce the long-standing political polarization in the country. The grooves in the political divide have become deeper and more solidified. A recent Gallup Poll showed that trust in government and nearly all other traditional institutions of our country are at very low levels. Only the military has a trust level that inspires confidence. While the Supreme Court is low, it exceeds that of the presidency. Trust in the Congress is appallingly low at 12%. Television news is not much higher, at 24%. The people and government should be pulling together during a crisis, but polarization is an integral part of this crisis period.

Figure 5-1.

Institution	Great deal/Quite a lot %
Military	72
Police	57
Organized religion	41
Supreme Court	40
Medical system	37
Public schools	36
Presidency	32
Banks	32
Banks	32
Organized Labor	28
Newspapers	27
Criminal Justice system	27
television news	24
Big Business	21
HMO's	19
News on Internet	16
Congress	12

(vol.) = Volunteered response; * Less than 0.5%
GALLUP POLL 2017

Events of recent years have all contributed to this lack of trust: the false premise of the Iraq war, the role of business and government in the financial crisis and Great Recession, a partisan health-care bill and subsequent gridlock in Congress, a politically polarized news media, on-going gun violence, shootings of unarmed African-Americans by police, and the vitriolic rhetoric of candidates during the presidential campaign. Members of each political party have their own views on each one of these issues. The fundamental issues plaguing America in Washington are a lack of effective leadership, shared purpose, and even a modicum of bi-partisan cooperation or civility.

Donald Trump framed his campaign around the difficulties facing the middle class with his "Make America Great Again" slogan. Perhaps he dropped the "Let's" from the front of Reagan's same campaign slogan from 1980 as Trump proclaimed that "I alone can fix it" at the Republican National Convention. He surprised everyone when he amassed enough electoral votes to become our 45th president. But "America First" should mean putting the entire country first, not the policies of one party, especially when that candidate lost the popular vote by nearly 3 million votes. His inauguration speech set forth the policies, budgets, and priorities of the victors and laid bare the splintered remains of the Democratic party and their progressive ideals, with no power to govern but a significant plurality of the voting populace behind them. Mark Lilla, a self-declared liberal, describes in his book *The Once and Future Liberal: After Identity Politics*, that "the reason the Democrats are losing ground...is because they have retreated into caves they have carved for themselves in the side of what once was a great mountain."[40]

The Women's March on Washington, D.C. the day after the inauguration dwarfed the new President's own festivities in both size and emotion. They sought to make clear that their gains over the past 50 years would be defended vocally. The same angst applies to the LBGT community, African-Americans, Hispanics and the remaining white men and women who voted for Hillary Clinton. The question is also whether economic and social progress will include all of these groups. We even heard echoes of Dwight D. Eisenhower's great initiatives of building the country's interstate highways, with a call to rebuild the nation's long-neglected infrastructure. The idea of building a massive wall along the U.S.-Mexican border and placing limitations on immigration was more controversial. Immigration has always been the bedrock of American principles and a source of economic growth. But attitudes haves shifted as the composition of immigrants have moved from white Europeans to Asians, Hispanics, and Muslim countries.

Strauss & Howe pointed out in *The Fourth Turning* in 1997, that immigration falls during a Crisis period and bottoms out during the High period. This Crisis period has borne out that prediction. They state that "the fall coincides with aggressive new efforts to protect the nation."[41] They accurately describe what has occurred both with immigration as well as the desire for travel bans on people from Muslim countries. There is a time for every purpose during each period in the cycle and immigration trends, like many others, are not linear. The national mood and the leaders we elect amplify the underlying sentiment, which changes with each new generation coming of age. Strauss & Howe add that immigration typically rises during an Awakening and peaks during the Unraveling period.

Trump called for "law and order" and offered unqualified support for our devoted members of law enforcement, while ignoring the senseless shootings of non-compliant, but unarmed, minorities by the few who would tarnish the honor of the badge. The crime rate has in fact been on a steady decline since 1980 and is at a fifty (50) year low! At the same time, he calls for large increases in defense spending, tax cuts for the wealthy, and cuts in discretionary spending but no policy solution for the massive entitlements that absorb a huge portion of the federal budget. The policies are consistent with the budgets enacted and large deficits produced by previous Republican administrations.

The country was yearning for change in 2016 after over 50 years of social and political turmoil, which pulsed through the country following the assassination of JFK in Dallas. Obama promised hope and change in 2008, but many were disappointed in the results. Trump focused his campaign on dissatisfied white voters. While Trump delivered an impassioned plea for unity in his state of the union address to Congress, his divisive campaign rhetoric, bombastic style and self-referencing focus left a majority of the nation feeling fearful and dejected. The political parties and their constituents remain divided over how to make any progress for the nation as a whole on health care, tax reform, federal spending, entitlement reform, as well as a variety of social issues.

While the electorate generally agrees that ISIS and North Korea pose a serious threat to national security, the country is divided along political lines over the motivations and need for a travel ban on people (Muslims) from seven countries in the Mid-East. The efficacy of such a ban might be questioned by any analysis or insights as to how or why the current vetting procedures are lacking in any way. It has not been demonstrated that immigrants or refugees already admitted from these countries have committed any hostile acts since being admitted. Objections have also been raised around the fact that the perpetrators of the 9/11 attacks were primarily from Saudi Arabia, which is not one of the countries on the temporary travel ban. The concern is that the travel ban itself is not really essential, but is largely a political overture to those who fear or resent Muslims. But immigration, or the resentment of those unlike the majority, is a common flash point in a crisis period. A tightening of vetting procedures could have just as easily been undertaken without a temporary ban, but would not be as public for Trump's purposes. A recent Supreme Court decision has allowed the executive order to go into effect, but with some specific criteria for allowing certain segments of applicants to be admitted. Bona fide connections to people already in the country or reasons to enter.

The news media remain focused largely on the twists and turns in the investigation over Russian attempts to influence the Presidential election by the hacking of Democrat's e-mails and the release of those through Wikileaks. To date there has not been any Wikileaks releases that have targeted improper government activities in Russia, itself without a functioning free press, casting huge doubt over their objectivity and real agenda. The U.S. media interest in this story was certainly fanned after revelations that several members of or advisers to the Trump campaign had numerous direct contacts with Russian officials during the campaign – after repeated denials that any contacts ever occurred. It has subsequently been revealed that the Trump organization was actively seeking approval from the Russian government for a new Trump Hotel in Moscow.

The first major casualty of the "Russian" issue was National Security Advisor Mike Flynn, who was forced to resign after admitting that he "misrepresented" his contacts with Russians as well as having discussed lifting sanctions.

He previously asserted these denials both publically and in private assurance with Vice-President Mike Pence, who vigorously defended Flynn on several Sunday talk shows. Subsequent to that, Mr. Flynn filed disclosure papers "retroactively" which indicated he had been an agent of the Turkish government for substantial monetary compensation. His legal troubles are far from over. Other former Trump campaign members or advisers who have since admitted to contacts with Russians include former campaign manager Paul Manafort, Attorney General Jeff Sessions, Carter Page, Jared Kushner and Donald Trump Jr. One of Trump's longtime confidantes and advisers, Roger Stone, has admitted to exchanging Twitter messages during the campaign with Guccifer 2.0, an account the U.S. intelligence community believes was used as a front by Russian hackers. Reuters reports that the communications between Russian officials and the Trump campaign began in April 2016—the same month Paul Manafort took over as Trump's campaign chairman. Soon after, a plank in the Republican platform supporting Ukraine was substantially watered down.

President Trump poured fuel on the Russian investigation fire when he fired F.B.I. Director Jim Comey, who was responsible for leading the investigation. Mr. Comey subsequently revealed his concern that President Trump had expressed his "hope" to Mr. Comey that the Flynn investigation would go away, in addition to asking Comey for his loyalty. Meanwhile, the F.B.I., Senate, and House investigations into Russian meddling in the 2016 elections continue, along with the related question of whether anyone in or around the Trump campaign may have colluded with the Russians to discredit Hillary Clinton. Special Counsel Robert Mueller is now leading the F.B.I. investigation. New information continues to come to light.

The government remains divided over how to reform health care after six years of Obamacare. Elements such as coverage of pre-existing conditions and ability of people under 26 to stay on their parents' plan are popular with Americans. With the Republicans controlling the White House and both houses of Congress, the ability to repeal and replace Obamacare is well within their power, but philosophical differences divide their own party. Negotiations were fractious in the House where the initial bill was defeated and a second version barely passed. The Republicans in the Senate have also struggled to pass a health-care bill, with at least six Republican Senators unwilling to vote for the initial bill, which was drafted behind closed doors with limited involvement. Without any participation or support by even the moderate Democrats in the process, as was the case with Republicans in passing Obamacare, any legislation passed will be subject to on-going criticism, and eventual change, when the government changes hands again. Senator John McCain returned to the senate floor for a crucial vote on health care in July, 2017 after having surgery for a blood clot and being diagnosed with brain cancer. He delivered an impassioned plea for bi-partisan cooperation on legislation and an end to the dysfunctional workings of Congress. He received a standing ovation. He demonstrably voted against the Trump bill.

The news media absolutely carries some responsibility for the decline in our political discourse over the past 30 years. The availability of 24/7 news on cable or through the internet on mobile devices has resulted in Americans being barraged by a constant stream of "breaking news," now tailored to each person's political affiliation on the cable channel of their choice or social media. Cable news outlets are desperate to fill their time slots and frequently do so by replaying (over and over) many un-newsworthy

segments. The polarization of our political system has led
to the fragmentation of vitriolic media on an individual
basis as well. Intelligent and objective journalism has
become a small niche in the world of most for-profit news
organizations driven by sound bites, ratings, and profit that
is based on building a brand around their anchors, rather
than objective news. The news used to be about the story
rather than the anchor, and anchors were trusted.

> *"Journalism is what we need to make democracy work."*
> Walter Cronkite

The confrontational atmosphere between the Trump
administration and the media is another element of the
current crisis mood. The media publicizes every actual or
perceived misstep by this administration and the executive
branch retaliates with denunciations of the media in
press briefings and emotional tweets by the president.
"Fake news" has become a new catch-phrase by the
administration to characterize any accusations against
or criticisms of the administration. Reckless use of that
term itself undermines our democracy and the free press,
although it might serve his own purposes.

The "war on terror" continues with ISIS having
replaced Al-Qaeda as the main perpetrator of violence
against civilians. The ubiquitous use of the term "terror" or
"terrorist" as the main descriptor of our enemy is preferred
by both the media and the government to dramatize the
conflict but serves no useful purpose in explaining who
we are fighting and why. The term is poignantly relevant
to the friends and families of those killed or maimed by
"terrorists," but adds nothing to the public discourse on
policy goals or strategy. Our battle is with radical Islamists
who reject western values and style of governance and
resent current and past military or colonial presence of

"non-believers" in Muslim countries. A caliphate with strict Sharia law and a traditional Islamist culture is the only path to heaven. The strategy for a broader description of our enemy in these terms would necessitate working with moderate Muslim elements in the U.S. and abroad to forge and pursue common goals. Terrorism cannot be defeated without fighting the message and beliefs that breed it.

An even greater threat is posed by the communist dictatorship in North Korea that continues its advance toward the development of a nuclear weapon as well as the means to deliver it on enemies near and far. Their development of nuclear energy, for future application to weapons, dates back to the 1980s. We have already seen the dangers of nuclear weapons in the hands of Pakistan and India, which would be much greater with a rogue state like North Korea, led by Kim Jong-un. China has been unwilling or unable to curtail the nuclear program of North Korea. President Trump is threatening further actions to punish and isolate North Korea. This could convince them to curtail their program or cause events to boil over into an active conflict. North Korea remains the most serious risk of the current crisis period. In a Pew Research Study conducted in June, 2017, several global threats were noted most frequently by Americans; ISIS, cyber-attacks, and North Korea. Respondents from both major parties agreed on the risks posed by these three threats. There was wide disagreement on the risks of three other global issues; Russia's power and influence, global climate change, and refugees from Syria and Iraq.

The economic outlook for the next 3-5 years seems much less problematic. The stock markets are at all-time highs, corporate profits are strong, unemployment is low, and interest rates are still low. The banking sector has announced plans to increase dividends and buy-back stock, having performed well in recent stress-tests administered by the Federal Reserve. The housing market has recovered from the precipitous fall that it took in 2007, wiping out billions in consumer home equity. Home prices are surging in many urban areas across the country where Millennials want to live. A mild recession is foreseeable in the next 2- 3 years. A major issue remains around the growing gap between the wealthy and all the rest. Since 1980, wages, and wealth, have soared for the Top 1% and lagged significantly for the remaining 99%. The stock market has performed well during this period, but rising incomes are needed to make investments. This issue was important in the 2016 election and will continue to be issues in 2018 and 2020, along with trade and jobs.

Figure 5-2.

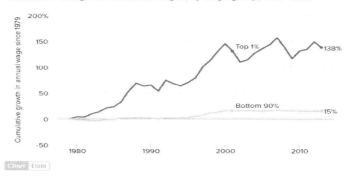

When it comes to the pace of annual pay increases, the top 1% wage grew 138% since 1979, while wages for the bottom 90% grew 15%

Cumulative change in real annual wages, by wage group, 1979–2013

All of this is meant to emphasize that while progress has been made, we are still embroiled in the Crisis period that began in 2001. In addition to the ongoing war against radical Islamists and the looming risk of conflict with

North Korea, the most tangible crisis remains, with the U.S. political system consumed with acrimony and polarization. With the 2016 elections behind us, the political landscape is set until 2019, with the Republicans firmly in charge. The outlook for the Democratic Party in the 2018 Senate elections is not good, but a chance exists to win back the House of Representatives. There has been no real change in the Democratic Party leadership or messaging following the upset victory by Donald Trump in 2016, other than the removal of Debbie Wasserman from the DNC. Nancy Pelosi remains as the minority leader in the House but a new generation waits in the wings. Qualified Gen X leaders need to step forward and Baby Boomers need to provide wise counselling, but make room for a new generation to lead. This new generation needs to be not as wedded to the fixed positions that Baby Boomers have been fighting over for more than 40 years, at the cost of actually getting anything done.

President Trump skillfully tapped into the unresolved grievances of white voters and swung typically blue states in the north to his side with a surge in white voter turnout. He recrafted the traditional Democratic message of economic populism and combined it with an anti-immigrant rhetoric that has been used effectively in America before. He won the strong Republican states with patented conservative calls for tax-cuts, an increase in military spending, an anti-abortion pledge, and the repeal and replacement of Obamacare. The Democrats will need strong leaders and an effective message to regain power in government. But anti-Trump sentiment is also running high, except with his core Republican base. Yet the key to winning for either party requires securing the vote of most Independents.

For the crisis mood to finally end, America's government will need to enter a new era, reminiscent of when the "likeable" Eisenhower replaced the unpopular Truman. In America's last High period, the political mood stabilized several years after the military conflict ended in 1945. The military drawdowns in Iraq and Afghanistan are much smaller than when WWII ended, but still symbolic of the transition from a Crisis mood to a High period. So, barring a major military conflict in the Middle East or North Korea, or another weather event during the upcoming 2017 hurricane season, only the American political crisis remains. (Hurricane Harvey hit Texas during this writing, soon followed by Irma and Maria).

While most would acknowledge that each political party benefits from some natural conflict with the other, the business of the country must (finally) be attended to. In focusing on relevant policy matters, a more civil tone must exist between the political parties as well as between government officials and the media. There should also be bi-partisan participation and support for major legislation. John Gardner notes in *Self-Renewal* that "in any society which functions effectively, some measure of consensus does exist"[42] but adds that "everyone does not have to agree in order for the consensus to be effective."[43] Our current political crisis can only end when President Trump has either changed his governing tone and style or is eventually replaced with someone who can effectively speak for and unite all Americans. Had Hillary Clinton won the 2016 election, the political dysfunction and polarization would have continued as well, and would only have ended when she left office. Regardless of which party the next President is from, the civility, decorum, and prestige that should reside with the presidency itself must be restored for an effective High period. That should occur with the 2020 elections.

In the meantime, the 2018 Congressional elections are the next major political event that could begin to form a new High period for America. The Democrats have an unlikely chance to win the Senate back in 2018 in light of the specific seats that are in play. They could even lose several Senate seats. But if history is any example, the Democrats have a real chance to retake the House, where all 435 seats are up for grabs in 2018. The Democrats would need to swing 24 seats to their side to gain a razor-thin majority. Coincidentally, that is the average number of seats that the party controlling the White House has lost in the mid-term elections since 1934. Given the polarizing and erratic behavior of President Trump and his low (40%) approval ratings, this seems within the realm of possibility for Democrats.

While the composition of the American electorate is still in the process of significant shifts to new, younger generations and an increasing number of Asian and Hispanic voters, the fact remains that the American voting electorate today is still predominantly white (70%), aged 40 and older (65%) and moderate (39%) according to *Business Insider* in a November, 2016 post-election analysis. Donald Trump won a decisive majority in each of these electoral groups in 2016. But women accounted for 52% of voters in 2016 compared to 48% for men and a majority (54%) of those women voted for Hillary Clinton. The black and Hispanic segments also voted overwhelmingly for Hillary. Many people ardently voted *against* Hillary Clinton in 2016, but she will not be a candidate moving forward. So President Trump and the Republicans cannot remain complacent about their success in 2016.

The potential for the current Republican majorities in Congress to craft a more conservative direction in key policy areas is significant. But wide divisions between the various Republican Congressional caucuses are making it difficult to pass major legislation solely within their own party, leaving some hope for bi-partisan collaboration with more moderate Democratic elements. After six years without any cooperation between the parties during Obama's presidency, progress is needed on legislation for health care, tax policy, and entitlement spending. Just getting some agreement on a budget and spending cap would go a long way in creating political and economic stability and helping to end this 16-year crisis mood.

In addition to the major legislative debates we face, the potential exists to change the composition of the Supreme Court over the next four years. This could determine the fate of the liberal social progress made over the past 60 years. The retirements of Justices Kennedy (80) and Ginsberg (84) could dramatically swing the court to a conservative majority for decades. While Justice Kennedy was appointed by President Reagan, he has frequently sided with the more liberal Justices in many cases. He is the only sitting judge who was approved by unanimous consent of the Senate (97-0), perhaps indicative of the balance he would bring to an otherwise divided court. Justice Ginsberg, perceived as a moderate when appointed by President Clinton in 1993, was approved 97-3. Justice Kennedy has recently resigned and Trump has appointed conservative Brett Kavanaugh as his replacement. Only Ginsberg continued tenure on the Court stands in the way of an overwhelming conservative majority.

Figure 5-3.

Trump nominee would restore conservative majority

Nominated by a Republican: John Roberts, Samuel Alito, Clarence Thomas, Anthony Kennedy, Neil Gorsuch

Nominated by a Democrat: Stephen Breyer, Elena Kagan, Sonia Sotomayor, Ruth Bader Ginsburg

BBC

The court has been frequently split 4-4 on major decisions with Justice Kennedy as the swing vote in deciding the case. The replacement of both Kennedy and Ginsberg with a conservative in the vein of Thomas or Gorsuch could swing the court to a 7-3 majority. While Kennedy has hinted that he is considering retirement in the near future, Ginsberg will need to be carried out on a stretcher before she would give President Trump the opportunity to replace her. If she is able to remain on the bench until 2020, her replacement on the Court will be another key issue in the Presidential election. The Republicans abolished the long-standing protocol that 60 votes were needed to approve a Supreme Court Justice when they pushed through Justice Gorsuch in 2017 with a simple majority, breaking the Democratic filibuster. This will have a major impact on the debate and approval process for all future nominations for the court. The best-case scenario for Democrats is that they take control of the Senate by 2020 and thus manage to maintain four seats on the court with Justices whose jurisprudence more closely approximates their own viewpoints. Social issues such as abortion rights, gun rights, gay rights, or "religious freedoms" could be affected by a heavily skewed conservative court.

The current Crisis period should end by 2020 or soon after. The Crisis has been turbulent but necessary, just as winter is necessary for spring. This will usher in a new American High period. Before that occurs, a final crisis could emerge in the form of a military or cyber conflict in the Middle East or Korea, an escalation of our political crisis at home, a serious attack by ISIS, or even a major weather event. In the absence of any of those more dire prospects, our political crisis should come to an end by 2020 and signal the start of a new, optimistic mood accompanied by cooperation, economic progress, and the nesting of Generation Y as parents and homeowners. The women's movement reached a crescendo in the last few years and will be a hallmark of the new mood of the High period.

Crosby, Stills and Nash's melodic song, Long Time Gone, touches on the exhaustion and hope that pervades the end of a long ordeal.

Chapter 6

New American High (2020 – 2038)

"The First Turning is a High, an upbeat era
of strengthening institutions and weakening
individualism, when a new civic order implants and
the old values regime decays."[44]

Figure 6-1.

Turning	Period	Families	Child Rearing	Gap in Gender Roles	Trust in Government	Voter Turnout	Social Priorities	New Gen Focus	Wars
First Turning	High	Strong	Loosening	Maximum	High	High	Max Community	do what works	restorative

When the crisis period ends around 2020, we will
enter a new High period. The 2020 Presidential election
could be the "single event" that marks the transition from
the Crisis to the High period. The country will be visibly
relieved when the crisis mood is over and is replaced with
a more unified country, more stable families and rising
economic security. We can expect to see evidence of that in
a cross-section of social attitudes and behaviors. Families
will be stronger, child rearing will loosen, the gap in gender
roles at their widest, institutions stronger, voter turnout and
trust in government at high levels, a sense of maximum
community and a focus on doing what works. John Gardner
noted in *Self-Renewal* that "just as beliefs and values are
susceptible to decay, so are they capable of regeneration."[45]

Figure 6-2.

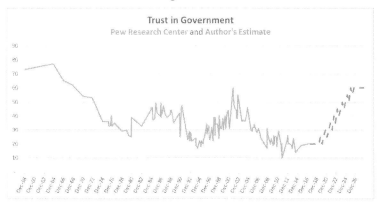

Here is a snapshot of some trends in social behavior that the new High period may offer:

- Marriage rates increase
- Divorce rates trend lower
- Fertility (birth) rates higher
- Abortion continues lower
- Crime rates remains low
- Voter turnout higher
- Trust in government increases

An ethos of "what's good for the group is good for the individual" will prevail. The conformist nature of the new High period will compare very favorably with the social, political and economic challenges of the past sixty years, albeit during a period of great progress. The younger generations will shape and form this mood. Even pop culture will be expected to provide a more supportive role in strengthening the social fabric. Aberrant public behavior in the (private) lives of public figures will not be tolerated. This trend had already taken hold in the Crisis period but will solidify during the High period. Leaders from all walks of life will be expected to be role models for the young. Along with this will be a much slower pace of social change, with little public appetite for new idealistic causes. Society is still busy digesting the ones we already have.

Figure 6-3.

	Order Period 2020 - 2038			
	Children	Young Adults	Mid-Life Adults	Elders
Generation	Gen A	Gen Z	Gen Y	Gen X
Archetype	Prophet	Artist	Hero	Nomad

The caring Artist archetype, over-protected as children, appear placid but advance values of pluralism, expertise and due-process. They gravitate toward consensus building and are comfortable with a conformist role.

Baby Boomers will gradually disappear from the demographic landscape, having made a permanent imprint on the American social order. Gen X will step forward as the new elders at age 60. Gen Y will move fully into middle age as they marry, raise families, and fill key roles in business, government, or service sectors. Gen Z will come of age as young adults and be dutiful in fulfilling their role. A new generation will be born starting in 2020, let's call them Gen A for now. These youth will grow up in the stable, protected, and positive new High period, but later come of age to drive the next Awakening period in 2038 or so.

Profile of Gen Z

Gen Z will be a unique new generation coming-of-age in 2020 with technology embedded in their daily life since birth. They were children during the Crisis period, when

Gen X and older millennial parents tightened parenting in response to a decline in traditional family order since the '70s. A group of 14-15-year-old boys expressed their generational perspectives to me during a recent visit to the local library. They explained that while they spent much of their time 'within' their own group, they could easily navigate relationships and communicate between the different ethnic groups that made up their school. The students quipped that "everyone got along and accepted each other."[46] They related to me that the blacks and Hispanics all used the 'n' word frequently, but that it was not meant (or taken) to be racist or anti-black. They all expressed that political correctness had "gone too far."[47] They believed that language was being simplified like "newspeak" in the novel *1984*. Fewer words said it all. They acknowledged that they were usually looking at their cell phones even when in groups and didn't make as much eye contact as they should. But "that's a problem for the next generation to solve."[48] They agreed parents were over-protective but that "it's a natural tendency for a generation to do the opposite of how it was when they were young."[49] While this group of young students is only a small microcosm of the generation, they were all very aware of current events and truly impressed me with their ability to discuss topics on multiple levels.

Ben Sasse, Republican Senator from Nebraska, sees the norms and experiences of the new generation as a threat to the American way of life. In this recent book, *The Vanishing Adult*, Sasse points to the over-protection of children by parents and the demotivating effects of government programs as contributing to their diminished capacity to survive in a global economy. He decries what he terms a passivity in the youth of today. What he and others may be noticing is the creation of the new "Silent" generation that may well be a "conformist" generation, but by no means are they ill-equipped in any way. I was also struck by the large group of Gen Y kids I saw at the local Apple store taking a summer class on using technology as a learning tool. The new generation will effectively provide the stabilizing social and professional role that the new High period will need them to serve.

Women and Family

While the High period may not herald the return to religion that Ben Sasse suggests is needed, marriage rates may well increase and birth rates may follow soon after. During the last High period, a young man who didn't marry might be criticized for immaturity. That charge has been leveled against Gen Y by some as they have delayed marriage, but a shift is in progress. Gen Z may even accelerate this trend as they marry sooner than their Gen Y elders. The cyclical return to a focus on community will reverse the negative trend we have witnessed during the past 40 years. Divorce rates will likely fall among Gen X and Gen Y couples as they personally experienced the damage that divorce inflicted on themselves and their peers. Marriages will be supported by a greater sense of responsibility and community.

Figure 6-4.

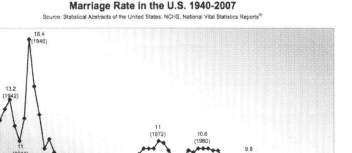

Abortion rates will continue to fall as unintended pregnancies among Gen Z decline, and birth control usage becomes even more embedded among singles as a normal part of their sexual behavior. Perhaps state legislatures looking to limit abortion will consider programs which help prevent unwanted pregnancies, particularly among the majority of abortion patients who are low-income or poor minorities, rather than making abortions more difficult to get. Democrats should consider ways to include the concept of "responsible choice" in their policy framework that places reasonable limits on the types of late-term abortions allowed, or even attract Democrats who may be pro-life. Finding common ground with moderates and even Republicans could serve to create a bi-partisan atmosphere. The collective mood of the High period will emphasize greater personal responsibility.

The new High period will be a resounding period for the advancement of women in all walks of society. Higher education, women in the workplace, marriage and birth rates are all closely intertwined issues. Women have been streaming to colleges and universities in greater numbers since the mid '90s and getting college degrees. They outpace men in pursuing and completing college. The "education gap" for men is even higher at the graduate degree level.

Figure 6-5.

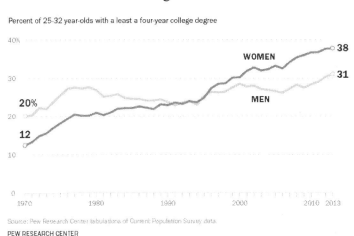

The greater flow of educated women into the workforce has had a beneficial effect on the "gender wage gap" between women and men. The gap has narrowed considerably over the past twenty years, with younger women seeing higher wages than "all workers." The Pew Research Center noted in 2012 that younger women (ages 25-34) earned 93% of what men did, up from about 85% in 2000. This gap should continue to narrow in the High period.

Figure 6-6.

The Narrowing of the Gender Wage Gap, 1980-2012

Median hourly earnings of women as a percent of men's

Note: Estimates are for civilian, non-institutionalized, full- or part-time employed workers with positive earnings. Self-employed workers are excluded.

Source: Pew Research Center tabulations of Current Population Survey data.

PEW RESEARCH CENTER

Women's ability to pursue careers and close the gender wage gap is inherently affected by their personal desire to have and care for children. A Pew Research Center study in 2013 showed they were more likely than men to work reduced hours, take a significant amount of time off or quit their jobs in order to care for a child or family member. Each of these can have a negative effect on a woman's ability to gain experience and earn more money over time. While men today may be more actively "sharing" in household or child-rearing duties, most of the responsibility still falls on women. Affordable child care is a greater challenge even for two-income families in the middle and lower economic classes.

Figure 6-7.

Percent saying they have ... in order to care for a child or family member

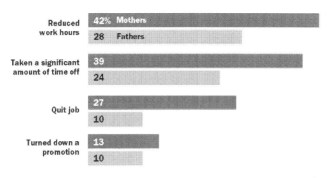

Note: "Fathers" and "mothers" include those with children of any age, including adult children (n=1,254).
Source: Pew Research Center survey, Oct. 7-27, 2013
PEW RESEARCH CENTER

The seismic shift that has occurred in the women's movement in 2017 and beyond will significantly affect the new High period. Women, families, and community will be at the heart of America's greater sense of stability. Sexual harassment has risen to a national conversation and a higher bar has been set for men's behavior inside the workplace or within relationships. I believe women will look back on this High period as a time when they realized many of their personal and professional goals, while effectively balancing marriage, children, work, and time for themselves. They will be treated with greater respect and equality. Companies that provide fair-paying jobs, consumer goods, services, or apps that make this easier for women will prosper.

Civil Rights

Ensuring the civil rights of all Americans should continue to be an enduring theme of the High period as a principle right of citizenship, regardless of identity group. The search for equal rights on the basis of ethnic group, gender, sexual orientation, and physical handicap has been the focus of social movements, legislation, and court battles over the past sixty years. While visible progress has been made, there is still more to be done to create a society where equal opportunity and treatment truly exists. Unlike an Awakening period, a High period is more about stability than idealistic causes, as legitimate as they may be. Existing legislation and court rulings, as well as the more pluralistic attitudes of younger generations, should serve to maintain the progress that has been made. But a significant shift to the right with new appointees on the Supreme Court could undermine progressive accomplishments.

The shootings of unarmed blacks by police officers has outraged many and led to the Black Lives Matter movement. The failure to convict most of the shooters has left many in the black community with the sense that equal protection and justice is not afforded them. The availability of cell phone and body cameras have provided the media and the American public an opportunity to witness many of the shootings. It is hard to imagine in most of them that the officer had a plausible reason to "fear for his life," especially when the victim was unarmed and running away. "Non-compliance" is not a death-penalty crime. At the same time, there are hundreds of blacks being killed by other blacks in Chicago and other cities. The Black Lives Matter group could advance their cause by taking a more visible and active stand in these neighborhoods to reduce the deaths of blacks there at the hands of other blacks.

The issue of justice for blacks morphed into a question of patriotism when several black football players "took a knee" during the national anthem. The debate had quieted down until President Trump chose to inflame it at a political rally in Alabama. There was a massive response by players and owners during the national anthem at games immediately after. Many in the public were outraged at what they regard as disrespect shown to the anthem, flag, and country. But there has been little discussion by the President or the public about the core issue which led to the protest in the first place. The public response is quite consistent with the mood that will prevail during the High period. During the Awakening period, protests against the war in Vietnam or for civil rights included burning the flag and using the black-gloved hand held high by black athletes during the national anthem at the Olympic Games in Mexico City in 1968. Neither of those protests was well-received by most people in America even during a counter-culture period. The response has been more critical during the current Crisis period and could be even more so in a conformist High period. As beneficiaries of our democracy, we must ask ourselves to evaluate and balance the cause or injustice behind a protest with the legal and peaceful form that the protest may take.

Former Supreme Court Justice Thurgood Marshall extolled the virtues of a democracy and the responsibility of it's citizens to protect it.

Crime

Crime rates are at a 50-year low and should remain low during the High period. Other negative social habits such as drug addiction and alcohol abuse should also trend lower. The current opioid crisis may well precipitate bi-partisan action to better control prescriptions and improve treatment. Conversely, the medical benefits of cannabis and the spread of legalization in some form to 39 states is reducing the public stigma around it, while generating much needed tax revenues for state and local government. Pressure is building for the Federal government to remove cannabis from the list of Schedule I drugs of the Controlled

Substances Act where it is listed alongside heroin, and eventually legalize it. The total crime rate should remain low through the High period, but could begin to increase as early as 2038.

Figure 6-8.

Of greater concern during the High period will be additional episodes of mass shootings by individuals. The past twenty years since the Columbine High School shootings has seen far too many tragic incidents. The problem needs to be addressed from multiple directions; mental-health care, family vigilance, sensible gun legislation, and more. A recent Gallup Poll shows that 55% of Americans feel that the laws covering the sale of firearms should be stricter. Our Second Amendment rights and the lives of innocent civilians should both be protected. Perhaps there is a bi-partisan approach that will satisfy most people.

Figure 6-9.

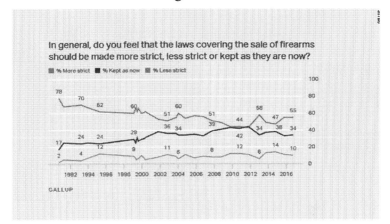

In general, do you feel that the laws covering the sale of firearms should be made more strict, less strict or kept as they are now?

GALLUP

Politics

The deep political divide that has marked the last 30 years will improve markedly as a sense of common purpose prevails, even though political differences will remain. Higher levels of trust in government will result from greater cooperation between the political parties on important national priorities. There are already signs that current and previous leaders of both parties see this as a necessity. Republican James A. Baker III and Democrat Andrew Young co-authored an editorial in the 8/31/17 issue of The Wall Street Journal titled "*Identity Politics are Tearing America Apart.*" They emphasize the main problem that "identity politics practiced by both political parties is eroding a core principle that Americans are, first and foremost, American."[50] Liberal Mark Lilla goes further to say "citizenship, the central concept of democratic politics, is a bond linking all members of a political society over time, regardless of their individual characteristics, giving them both rights and duties."[51] Baker and Young

139

add that there is a need for all politicians to "restrain their rhetoric and practice the lost art of compromise."[52] John Gardner emphasizes that "a pluralistic society wisely seeks to establish its consensus in the middle depths, the ideals of freedom, equality of opportunity, the conception of the worth and dignity of the individual, the idea of justice, the dream of brotherhood."[53] A wider recognition of these viewpoints could positively contribute to bi-partisan cooperation on taxes, health care, education, government spending, and other areas. Active members of both Gen X and Gen Y can force this shift through their focus on team-work and getting things done, and with the type of people they vote for in upcoming elections. Their generational preference for principles of pluralism will advance cooperation among all groups.

A "public purpose" period in the Schlesinger political cycle model is also set to begin in 2020. This will be a shift from the 1950s when the High period coincided with a "private interest" period favoring business. A "public purpose" period could include more government investment in infrastructure projects, resolution of entitlements, and greater bipartisan cooperation on other issues. As these political cyclic periods are moods and are not absolutes, they will be just another influence on the High period itself. The "public interest" period should serve to balance the "free-market" aspect of the High period with the government acting to protect the interests of the broader public as well.

Figure 6-10.

Theory of Cycles	2000	2005	2010	2015	2020	2025	2030	2035
Strauss & Howe - Generational Cycles								
High						High		
Awakening								
Unraveling								
Crisis		Crisis						
Schlesinger - Political								
Public Purpose						Public		
Private interest				Private				
Klingberg - Foreign Policy								
Extrovert	Extrovert							
Introvert						Introvert		

As of the 2016 election, the Pew Research Center reported that Millennials and Gen X already constituted 56% of the eligible voters. That balance will shift even higher by 2020. According to a May, 2017 Pew Research Center study, voter turnout by Millennials in 2016 was only 49%, well below that for other generations. Voter turnout by Gen Y should shift significantly higher for the 2020 election, along with their impact on the outcome. Among registered voters, Millennials tilt strongly in favor of Democrats according to a September, 2016 Pew Research Center study while Boomers and Gen X are very closely split between Democrats and Republicans.

Figure 6-11.

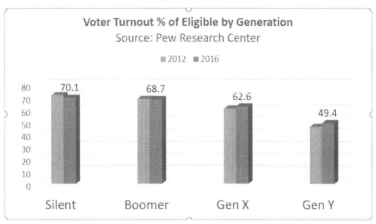

President Trump may well face a challenge in the
Republican primaries in 2020, as President Ford did from
Ronald Reagan in 1976. Although he won the nomination
in 2016 by positioning himself as an outsider who could
change Washington, he will be judged by his actual record
in the 2020 election. With his approval ratings still below
40% (chart below), only his base is keeping his rating from
going lower. That provides an opportunity for another
Republican to appeal to other segments of voters in the
primaries. Perhaps he will be the sixth President since
1948 *not* to secure a second term, compared with the six
Presidents who did get re-elected to a full second term.

Figure 6-12 President Trump Approval Ratings

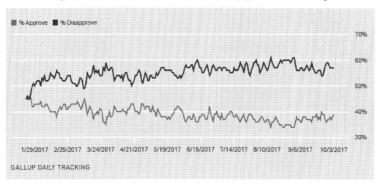

Trump won only 41% of voters who described themselves as "moderates," according to a 2016 Roper Exit Pools, but that was enough to win the election. "Moderates" accounted for 39% of the voters, more than either liberals (26%) or conservatives (35%) according to those exit polls. The "lost middle" will continue to reassert themselves in the new High period. It remains to be seen which party will capture their support in upcoming elections.

Another question is who will run in the primaries for the Democratic nomination. The cycles of history suggest that the most electable candidate for the Democrats for the coming High period would be a moderate. A (male or female) veteran of the Afghan or Iraq wars would have broad appeal, like Eisenhower had in 1952 when he delivered a crushing defeat to Democrat Adlai Stevenson. A left-wing liberal would not secure broad, national appeal in the country on the doorstep of a High period. A political moderate candidate from Gen X or Gen Y would be a formidable challenge to Trump in 2020, who will be 74 by then. Another key to victory for either party will be who appeals best to independent voters, which constituted 31% of voters in 2016 of which Trump received 48%. In 2020, Baby Boomers will be turning 75. By 2020 or soon after, Harry Reid, Mitch McConnell, and Nancy Pelosi (all members of the Silent generation) should have yielded their positions of power in Congress to younger generations. The mood and dynamic in Congress will certainly shift with younger leadership.

One of the most significant issues that will affect the political make-up of local, state and federal government in the new High period will be the changing demographics of the country. Demographics, as well as voter turnout, will significantly affect the upcoming national elections in 2020, and into the new High period. According to the Pew Research Center, Hispanics will account for 15.6% of the eligible voters by 2030, up from 11.1% in 2012. In light of recent studies that show that nearly 70% of Hispanic voters identify as Democratic, or leaning toward Democrats, that translates to an additional 11 million votes for Democratic candidates. By the middle of the High period in 2030, white voters will drop to 64% of the electorate with minorities constituting over 36%.

Figure 6-13.

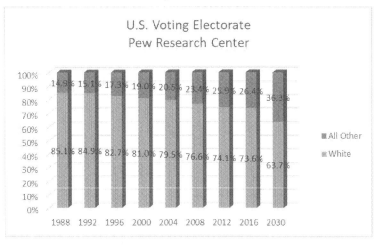

Actual voter turnout will be a crucial factor in realizing the power that comes with that potential. Voter turnout among Hispanics has been steadily increasing the past 16 years, reaching 45% in 2016, but well below the 65% for whites. Voter turnout by Blacks surged to 69% in 2008 -- even exceeding white turnout -- and helped to elect Barak Obama. After re-electing Obama in 2012 with a 67% turnout, Black turnout dropped measurably to 60%.

Figure 6-14.

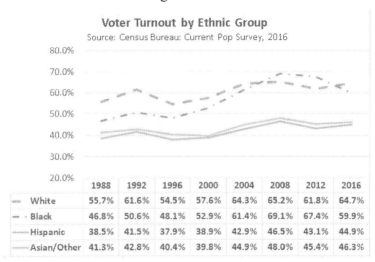

	1988	1992	1996	2000	2004	2008	2012	2016
White	55.7%	61.6%	54.5%	57.6%	64.3%	65.2%	61.8%	64.7%
Black	46.8%	50.6%	48.1%	52.9%	61.4%	69.1%	67.4%	59.9%
Hispanic	38.5%	41.5%	37.9%	38.9%	42.9%	46.5%	43.1%	44.9%
Asian/Other	41.3%	42.8%	40.4%	39.8%	44.9%	48.0%	45.4%	46.3%

The 2016 election was a vivid reminder that, although the white population as a percent of the electorate has declined since 1988, the whites still constitute a significant percentage of the electorate and they can affect the election when they turn out to vote. As their share of the total voting electorate has fallen to 73% in 2016 from 85% in 1988, white voter turnout has steadily risen over the past 30 years. This trend should continue as white voters understandably seek to maintain some influence on the direction the country takes, whether they be progressives or conservatives. Democrats should have learned a lesson from the 2016 election and articulate a message that will resonate with moderate white, male voters.

Figure 6-15.

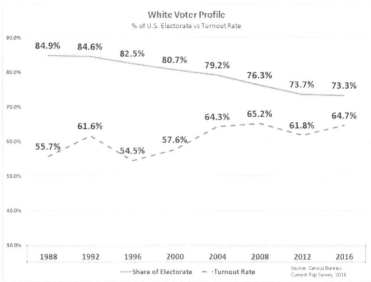

When looking at voter turnout compared with the period of the cycle, there appears to be a pattern. Looking back over the past 150 years, voter turnout is higher in the High periods, declines during the Awakening and Unraveling periods and increases again during the Crisis period. Total voter turnout was 60% in the 2016 election as white voter turnout increased. We are approaching the high voter turnout levels seen during the last Crisis period which extended through the High period until 1968.

Figure 6-16.

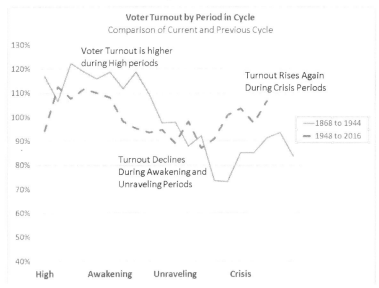

I believe we will continue to see high voter turnout through 2020 and into the next decade as the electorate presses for effective government action on major issues. It seems unlikely that we will see a return to the 75-80% voter turnout levels witnessed from 1868 – 1888, but they could reach 65%. A major difference affecting voter turnout compared with the 1800s is the inclusion of blacks and women among eligible voters. While women were granted the right to vote in 1920, blacks were effectively blocked from voting by a myriad of state restrictions until the Voting Rights Act of 1965 was passed. In Mississippi, black voter turnout increased from 6% in 1964 to 59% in 1969.

The make-up of religious affiliation will be shifting in the next 20 years and will have a major impact on election results and public policy. The percentage of the electorate identifying themselves as Christian has dropped from 78% to 70% from 2007 to 2014. As a significant percentage of Hispanics (70%) are Catholic, that could begin to reverse as the population reaches voting age. Meanwhile, the percentage identifying themselves as "unaffiliated" with any religion has increased from 16% to 23% in the same seven years, driven by greater numbers of Gen X (23%) and Millennials (35%). This compares with much lower "unaffiliated" levels for the Silent generation (10%) and Baby Boomers (16%). Strauss & Howe describe a High period as one where the culture shifts from inner directed (spiritual) to outer focused (civic). This decline in religious affiliation may have an effect on voter attitudes during the High period on religious issues such as abortion and gay rights.

Figure 6-17.

Decline in Those Identify as Christian and Increase in Unaffiliated Driven by Changing Mix of Younger Generations								
	Total U.S.			Generation				
Religious Affiliation	2007	2014	chg	Silent	Baby Boomers	Gen X	Older Gen Y	Younger Gen Y
Christian	78.4%	70.6%	-7.8%	85%	78%	70%	57%	55%
Non-Christian	4.7%	5.9%	1.2%	4%	5%	6%	8%	8%
Unaffiliated	16.1%	22.8%	6.7%	10%	16%	23%	34%	36%
Don't Know/No Answer	0.8%	0.6%	-0.2%	0.6%	0.6%	0.6%	0.6%	0.6%
Total	100%	100%		100.0%	100.0%	100.0%	100.0%	100.0%

Pew Research Center
2014 Religious Landscape Study

Foreign Policy

Wars during a High period are characterized as "restorative" by Strauss and Howe. For example, as Russia was emerging from their own Crisis period, which started with the collapse of the Soviet Union in 1991, they became more assertive in areas that were previously part of the

U.S.S.R. They invaded Georgia in 2008 and the Ukraine in 2014, reclaiming the Crimea peninsula which was ceded to the Ukraine SSR in 1954 by Khrushchev after 170 years of Russian rule. For the U.S., any unresolved issues from the Crisis period may be a flash point for further conflict. This would certainly include limited military action in the Middle East against ISIS or Al Qaeda. It may also include a more concerted push-back against Russia in Eastern Europe or China in the South China Sea. During the last High period (1945 – 1963), the major conflict was the Korean War, with troop deployments reaching nearly 600,000 soldiers, but coincided with an "extroverted" foreign policy cycle and was precipitated by the North Korean invasion of the South. At that time, the USSR was their major backer and the invasion was launched with the permission of Stalin in an attempt to unify the country under Communist rule. China has since become North Korea's main benefactor and ally. North Korea is currently on a path to secure nuclear weapons, which neither China nor the U.S. has been able to discourage or prevent with sanctions. The situation in North Korea could boil over in the current Crisis period or in the High period. But the mood will be "introverted" by 2020, unlike the "extroverted" foreign policy mood in 1950, when the Korean War started. Also, China will not want to see their economic growth or regional influence damaged by a war on the Korean peninsula.

This "introverted" foreign policy mood will serve as a limiting influence on major U.S. military actions in the High period. The last introvert period was 1970 – 1990, which clearly saw a less aggressive period of foreign military action after the Vietnam War. A continued strategy of "America First" would reinforce that introverted foreign policy and minimize major military interventions unless directly provoked or a clear national security threat was present. The U.S. will continue to exert their foreign-policy goals through negotiations, backed by a strong military and robust economy. We will expand our ability to utilize cyber warfare, drones, robotics, and Special Forces as needed to counter comparable threats.

Figure 6-18.

Theory of Cycles	2000	2005	2010	2015	2020	2025	2030	2035
Strauss & Howe - Generational Cycles								
High						High		
Awakening								
Unraveling								
Crisis		Crisis						
Schlesinger - Political								
Public Purpose						Public		
Private interest				Private				
Klingberg - Foreign Policy								
Extrovert	Extrovert							
Introvert						Introvert		

Conclusion

Cycles are an integral part of our planet and our human existence. Nature thrives on cycles of birth, maturation, decay, and death. Seasons follow a perennial cycle of spring, summer, fall and winter. A human life has its own cycle that mirrors the four seasons and lasts about twenty years each. Those periods also correspond with the cohorts of a generation. Similar cycles exist in our political, economic, and foreign affairs. This has been a story of the cycles of social change in our country and the overlay of the generations on those cycles as actors within and instigators of that social change.

While time clearly appears to move in a linear fashion, with one day following the next and the months and years occurring in succession, there is also a rhythm to our lives that is cyclical. It is within the seasons of that cycle that each generation comes of age and imprints their unique perspective on the direction of society. The periods within the cycle can reflect the mood and persona of the same period in a previous cycle. They are related to the constant unfolding of the great human experience in the universe. The cyclical change in the persona of each generation serves as a natural corrective to swings in social order that have gone too far in one direction or another. Shifts in the social mood in a country cannot be forseen when looked at through a linear prism. Cyclical changes, like curves in the road ahead, are not fully experienced until you're into and beyond them.

This generational social cycle contains four distinct periods of High, Awakening, Unraveling, and Crisis. It has repeated itself many times in the history of America. The mood of each period and the persona of each generation shape the lens through which we see events that occur during those periods and how we react to them.

Figure 6-19.

We will soon complete the fourth and last period in the full cycle that began in 1945 with the end of WWII and has coursed its way through the tumultuous '60s, the culture wars of the '80s, and finally the terrorism, deep recession, and political polarization of the first two decades of the new millennium. Each of these unique periods in our recent history was necessary, even if painful, for our growth. Just as we all experience successes and failures along our path in life, so does society as a whole. There is no right or wrong in the changing of the seasons. The crisis period will end soon and a new High period will be ushered in. Spring is just around the corner. An exhausted public will be relieved and gladly settle into a conforming but more cooperative and stable period.

The new mood of the High period will be driven by the Millennials advancing to mid-life, guided by pragmatic Gen X, and supported by dutiful, young Gen Z. A greater spirt of cooperation and community will prevail. Marriage rates will increase, divorce will continue to trend lower, birth rates will increase, abortion rates will trend lower, voter turnout will increase, and trust in government will improve significantly. The High period will usher in a memorable time of American Renewal.

Enjoy the rest, but remember that nature will demand the continuation of the cycle and the hot days of summer will follow in due time. Our social order follows its own natural cycle.

John Mayer ponders in 2006 what might occur when Gen Y finally steps forward to lead the country in Waiting On The World to Change.

Bibliography

Preface

Lisa Bannon, *Why Girls and Boys Get Different Toys*, The Wall Street Journal, Feb. 14, 2000

Bruce Springsteen, *Born to Run*, Simon & Schuster, New York, 2016

Introduction

John W. Gardner, *Self-Renewal The Individual and the Innovative Society*, W.W. Norton & Company, New York, 1981

Pew Research Center, *Trust in Government* 1958 - 2016

Arthur M. Schlesinger, Jr. *The Cycles of American History*, Houghton Mifflin Company, Boston, 1986

William Strauss and Neil Howe, *Generations: The History of America's Future 1584 to 2069*, Harper Perennial, New York, 1991

William Strauss and Neil Howe, *The Fourth Turning: An American Prophecy*, Broadway Books, New York, 1997

Frank L. Klingberg, *Cyclical Trends in American Foreign Policy Moods*, University Press of America Inc, Lanham, 1983

Amy Zalman, PhD *The History of Terrorism*, ThoughtCo. March 23, 2017

Francis Fukuyama, *The Great Disruption Human Nature and the Reconstitution of Social Order*, Touchstone, New York, 1999

Kimberley Amadeo, *GDP Growth by Year (1929 – 2016)*, Bureau of Economic Analysis

Chapter 1 – America's Last High Period (1945 – 1963)

Joseph Goulden, *The Best Years 1945-50*, Athenum, New York, 1976

William O'Neill, *The American High: The Years of Confidence 45-60*, The Free Press, New York, 1986

David Halberstam, *The Fifties*, Villard Books, New York, 1993

David Halberstam, *The Best and the Brightest*, Random House, New York, 1969

Robert J. Samuelson, *The Good Life and Its Discontents: The American Dream in the Age of Entitlement*, Vintage Books, New York, 1995

Robert J. Donovan, *Conflict and Crisis; The Presidency of Harry S. Truman, 1945-1948*, W.W. Norton & Company, New York, 1977

Robert Ellwood, *The Fifties Spiritual Marketplace: American Religion in a Decade of Conflict,* Rutgers University Press, 1997

The Postwar Period Through the 1950s, Encyclopedia of American Social History, 1993,

Chapter 2 – Awakening Period (1963 – 1980)

Gen Y shaped, not stopped, by tragedy, USA Today April 18, 2007 page 1D

George F. Kennan, *Memoirs 1925 – 1950,*Little, Brown and Company, Boston, 1967

Francis Fukuyama, *The Great Disruption Human Nature and the Reconstitution of Social Order*, Touchstone, New York, 1999

Steven Pinker, *Decivilization in the 1960s from The Better Angels of Our Nature*, Viking Penguin, 2011

Election Results, 270towin.com

U.S. Troop Deployments 1950-2015, Source: DOD
    compiled by Tim Kane,
U.S Troop Levels in Vietnam, Department of Defense
Voter Turnout in U.S. Elections, compiled by Gehert Peters
    from Federal Election Commission data.

Chapter 3 – Unraveling Period (1981 – 2001)

San Francisco Examiner, *Evolution of a Voter*, April 16,
    1984 page 38
Median Income of Married Couple Families
Election Results, 270towin.com

Chapter 4 – Crisis Strikes America (2001 – 2017)

Iconoculture Consumer Insights, *Millennial Ties That
    Bind*, 2014
Millennials – Breaking the Myth, Nielsen, 2014
Time Magazine, *The Greatest Generation*, May, 2013
Median Age at First Marriage 1890 – 2010, U.S. Census
U.S. Birth Rate 1910 – 2015, CDC/NVSS
Marriage Rates in the U.S. 1940-2007, Statistical Abstract
    of the U.S., NCHS
U.S. Divorce Rates Peak Around 1980, National Marriage
    Project, University of Virginia
Pew Research Center, *Survey on Parenting*
Wall Street Journal, *Television Habits that Put Family
    First*, June 13, 2015
Murder Rates in the U.S., FBI UCS Annual Crime Reports
Total Crime in the U.S., From: FBI UCS Annual Crime
    Reports
Pew Research Center, Gun Policy
Peter Hopkirk, *The Great Game*, Kodansha America, New
    York, 1994

U.S. Troop Levels in Afghanistan and Iraq 2001-2015,
Dept. of Defense
U.S. Troop Levels in Afghanistan 2001- 2016, Dept. Of
Defense
Unemployment in the U.S., Bureau of Labor Statistics
Pew Research Center, Study on Bi-Partisan Support, 2015
Samuel P. Huntington, *The Clash of Civilizations:
Remaking of World Order*, Touchstone, Simon &
Schuster, New York, 1996
Abigail Abrams, *Divorce Rates in US Drops to Nearly
40-Year Low*, Time.com Dec. 4, 2016
National Center for Health Statistics, *Marriage Rates in the
U.S.*, 2010
Katie Park/NPR, *U.S. Abortion Rates at Lowest Recorded
Point,* Guttmacher Institute
Population Reference Bureau Archives: 2012 Mark Mather,
The Decline in U.S. Fertility
Peggy Noonan, *What's Become of the American Dream*,
The Wall Street Journal, April 8-9, 2017
Jeff Fromm and Christie Garton, *Marketing to Millennials*,
AMACON, New York, 2013

Chapter 5 – Crisis and Resolution (2017 – 2020)

Gallup Poll, Trust in Institutions, 2017
Pew Research Center, Study on Global Threats, June, 2017
Wage Growth 1980-2010, Economic Policy Institute
Business Insider, 2016 Election Analysis, Nov, 2016
U.S. Supreme Court Justices by Appointment, BBC, 2017

Chapter 6 – New American High Periods (2020 – 2039)

Pew Research Center, *Study of Voter Turnout by
Generation*, May, 2017

Pew Research Center, *Study on Party Preference by Generation*, Sept, 2016

Roper Exit Polls, 2016 Election

Marriage Rates in U.S. 1970-2013, U.S. Wedding Forecast, Demographic Intelligence

Pew Research Center, *U.S. Voting Electorate by Ethnic Group*

Voter Turnout by Ethnic Group, Census Bureau, Current Population Survey, 2016

White Voter Profile, Census Bureau, Current Population Survey, 2016

Historical Voter Turnout in U.S. 1868-2016, compiled by Lyn Ragsdale and Gehert Peters, Vital Statistic on the Presidency and Federal Election Commission

Pew Research Center, *2014 Religious Landscape*

Ben Sasse, *The Vanishing American Adult*, St. Marten's Press, New York, 2017

Mark Lilla, *The Once and Future Liberal, After Identity Politics*, Harper Collins, New York 2017

Notes

1   John Gardner, *Self Renewal*, page 2
2   John Gardner, Self Renewal, page xiv
3   Arthur M. Schlesinger, Jr. *The Cycles of American History*, page 27
4   Frank L. Klingberg, *Cyclical Trends in American Foreign Policy Moods*, page 1
5   Frank Klingberg, *Cyclical Trends in American Foreign Policy Moods*, page 1
6   Francis Fukayama, *The Great Disruption*, page 6
7   William Strauss and Neil Howe, *Generations,* page 34
8   William Strauss and Neil Howe, *The Fourth Turning*, page 18
9   Ibid page 3
10 Ibid page 3
11 Ibid page 3
12 Ibid page 3
13 Wikipedia, List of American Superhero films since 2000 by Marvel Comics or DC Comics. April, 2018.
14 William Strauss and Neil Howe, *The Fourth Turning,* page 3
15 William Strauss and Neil Howe, *Generations*, page 281
16 Joseph Goulden, *The Best Years 1945-1950*, page 427
17 Ibid, page 427
18 William L. O'Neill, *American High The Years of Confidence 1945 – 1960*, page 44
19 David Halberstam, *The Fifties*
20 George Kennan, *Memoirs 1925-1950*, page 359
21 Ibid, page 358
22 Kennedy Inauguration Speech,
23 Wikipedia, Kennedy Inauguration Speech, January 1961.

24. William Strauss and Neil Howe, *The Fourth Turning*, page3
25. Kennedy Inauguration speech
26. *Cool Hand Luke*, Warner Brothers, 1967
27. The Graduate
28. Ibid
29. Presidential Crime Commission, 1967 page 6
30. Steven Pinker, *Decivilization of the 1960's*, Volume 2, Issue 2 July, 2013
31. William Strauss and Neil Howe, *The Fourth Turning*, (New York, 1997), page3.
32. William Strauss and Neil Howe, *The Fourth Turning*, page 208
33. William Strauss and Neil Howe, *The Fourth Turning*, page 103
34. George Kennan, *Memoirs 1925-1950*, page 364
35. William Strauss and Neil Howe, *The Fourth Turning*, page 3
36. PEW Research Center study, *Millennials, A Portrait of Generation Next*, February 2010, page 1
37. Ibid, page 2
38. CEB (Corporate Executive Board Company), Iconoculture Consumer Insights, *The Millennial Ties That Bind,* 2014, page 3
39. The Nielsen Company, *Millennials – Breaking The Myths*, 2014, page 3
40. Mark Lilla, *The Once and Future Liberal*, 2017, page 11
41. William Strauss and Neil Howe, *The Fourth Turning*, 1997, page 113
42. John W. Gardner, *Self-Renewal, The Individual and the Innovative Society*, 1981, page 117
43. Ibid, page 118
44. William Strauss and Neil How, *The Fourth Turning*, 1997, page 3

45 John W. Gardner, *Self-Renewal*, page xiv
46 Monterey High School Student interview at Monterey Public Library, November 2017
47 Ibid
48 Ibid
49 Ibid
50 James A. Baker and Andrew Young, The Wall Street Journal, *Identity Politics Are Tearing America Apart*, August 31, 2017, Sec. A, page 17
51 Mark Lilla, *The Once and Future Liberal*, 2017, page 88
52 Op Cit.
53 John W. Gardner *Self-Renewal*, page 118